DETECTION OF DEVELOPMENTAL PROBLEMS IN CHILDREN

DETECTION OF DEVELOPMENTAL PROBLEMS IN CHILDREN

A Reference Guide for Community Nurses and Other Health Care Professionals

edited by

Marilyn J. Krajicek, R.N., M.S.
Alice I. Tearney, R.N., M.S.

John F. Kennedy Child Development Center
University of Colorado Medical Center

University Park Press
Baltimore · London · Tokyo

UNIVERSITY PARK PRESS
International Publishers in Science and Medicine
Chamber of Commerce Building
Baltimore, Maryland 21202

Typeset by The Composing Room of Michigan, Inc.
Manufactured in the United States of America by Universal Lithographers,
Inc., and The Optic Bindery Incorporated

Library of Congress Cataloging in Publication Data

Main entry under title:

Detection of developmental problems in children.

Includes index.
1. Children—Medical examinations. 2. Child de-
velopment—Testing. 3. Pediatric nursing. I. Krajicek,
Marilyn J. II. Tearney, Alice I. [DNLM: 1. Child
development deviations—Diagnosis—Nursing texts. WY159
D479]
RJ50.D47   618.9'2007'5   76-49651
ISBN 0-8391-0949-0

CONTENTS

Embryonic development chart vi
Fetal development chart viii
Preface xi
Acknowledgments xii
Contributors xiii

I. NURSING ASSESSMENTS—SCREENING FOR DEVELOPMENTAL
   PROBLEMS
   A. Home Visit—As Related to a Diagnostic Clinic
      Evaluation / *Alice I. Tearney, R.N., M.S.* 1
   B. Background Information / *Marilyn J. Krajicek, R.N., M.S.* ...7
   C. Physical Examination of the Child / *Elna Cain, R.N., M.S.* ..15
   D. Use of Screening Tools / *Paula Roberts, R.N., M.S.* 31
II. THE EMBRYONIC PATIENT: AN OPPORTUNITY FOR
   THE PREVENTION OF DEVELOPMENTAL PROBLEMS /
   Cole Manes, M.D. 47
III. GENETIC DISORDERS / *Marie-Louise Lubs, Ph.D.* 55
IV. THE HIGH RISK INFANT / *Annette Lansford, M.D.* 79
V. NORMAL MOTOR DEVELOPMENT IN THE INFANT /
   Linda Lord, R.P.T., M.P.H. 89
VI. VISION SCREENING / *Cyndi Thero* 101
VII. GUIDELINES FOR HEARING SCREENING OF THE INFANT,
   PRESCHOOL, AND SCHOOL-AGE CHILD /
   Marion P. Downs, M.A. 111
VIII. SPEECH AND LANGUAGE DEVELOPMENT /
   Kathleen Bryant, M.A. 131
IX. NUTRITION AND THE CHILD / *Philomena Lomena, M.S.* ...141
X. FAMILIES WITH CHILDREN AT RISK FOR SCHOOL
   PROBLEMS / *William J. van Doorninck, Ph.D.* 151
XI. BEHAVIOR MODIFICATION: USE WITH CHILDREN /
   Nancy Matthews Weaver, B.S., M.S., and
   Marilyn J. Krajicek, R.N., M.S. 161
XII. ROLE OF THE PUBLIC HEALTH NURSE IN CASES OF
   CHILD ABUSE / *Brian G. Fraser, J.D.* 177
XIII. ON BECOMING A HELPER / *Jane E. Chapman, R.N., Ph.D.* ..193
   Index 199

EMBRYONIC DEVELOPMENT

AGE days	LENGTH mm.	STAGE Streeter	GROSS APPEARANCE	C.N.S.	EYE	EAR	FACE
4		III	Blastocyst				
8	.1	IV	embryo, trophoblast, endometrium				
12	.2	V	ectoderm amnionic sac endoderm, yolk sac				
18	1	VIII	ant. head fold body stalk heart	Enlargement of anterior neural plate			
22	2	X early somites	foregut allantois	Partial fusion neural folds	Optic evagination	Otic placode	Mandible Hyoid arches
26	4	XII 21-29 somites		Closure neural tube Rhombencephalon, mesen., prosen. Ganglia V VII VIII X	Optic cup	Otic invagination	Fusion, mand. arches
32	7	XIV		Cerebellar plate Cervical and mesencephalic flexures	Lens invagination	Otic vesicle	Olfactory placodes
38	11	XVI		Dorsal pontine flexure Basal lamina Cerebral evagination Neural hypophysis	Lens detached Pig-mented retina	Endolymphic sac Ext. auditory meatus Tubotym-panic recess	Nasal swellings
43	17	XVIII		Olfactory evagination Cerebral hemisphere	Lens fibers Migration of retinal cells Hyaloid vessels		Choana, Prim. palate
47	23	XX		Optic nerve to brain	Corneal body Mesoderm No lumen in optic stalk		
51	28	XXII			Eyelids	Spiral cochlear duct Tragus	

EMBRYONIC DEVELOPMENT CHART

The embryonic ages for Streeter's stages XII - XXIII have been altered in accordance with the human data from Iffy, L. et al: Acta Anat. 66 : 178, 1967

EXTREMITIES	HEART	GUT, ABDOMEN	LUNG	UROGENITAL	OTHER
					Early blastocyst with inner cell mass and cavitation (58 cells) lying free within the uterine cavity
					Implantation Trophoblast invasion Embryonic disc with endoblast and ectoblast
		Yolk sac			Early amnion sac Extraembryonic mesoblast, angioblast Chorionic gonadotropin
	Merging mesoblast anterior to prechordal plate	Stomatodeum Cloaca		Allantois	Primitive streak Hensen's node Notochord Prechordal plate Blood cells in yolk sac
	Single heart tube Propulsion	Foregut		Mesonephric ridge	Yolk sac larger than amnion sac
Arm bud	Ventric. outpouching Gelatinous reticulum	Rupture stomatodeum Evagination of thyroid, liver, and dorsal pancreas.	Lung bud	Mesonephric duct enters cloaca	Migration of myotomes from somites
Leg bud	Auric. outpouching Septum primum	Pharyngeal pouches yield parathyroids, lat. thyroid, thymus Stomach broadens	Bronchi	Ureteral evag. Urorect. sept. Germ cells Gonadal ridge Coelom, Epithelium	Rathke's pouch
Hand plate, Mesench. condens. Innervation	Fusion mid. A-V canal Muscular vent. sept.	Intestinal loop into yolk stalk Cecum Gallbladder Hepatic ducts Spleen	Main lobes	Paramesonephric duct Gonad ingrowth of coelomic epith.	Adrenal cortex (from coelomic epithelium) invaded by sympathetic cells = medulla Jugular lymph sacs
Finger rays, Elbow	Aorta Pulmonary artery Valves Membrane ventricular septum	Duodenal lumen obliterated Cecum rotates right Appendix	Tracheal cartil.	Fusion urorect. sept. Open urogen. memb., anus Epith. cords in testicle	Early muscle
Clearing, central cartil.	Septum secundum			S-shaped vesicles in in nephron blastema connect with collecting tubules from calyces	Superficial vascular plexus low on cranium
Shell, Tubular bone				A few large glomeruli Short secretory tubules Tunica albuginea Testicle	Superficial vascular plexus at vertex

EMBRYONIC DEVELOPMENT CHART

FETAL DEVELOPMENT

AGE weeks	LENGTH cm. C-R	LENGTH cm. Tot.	WT. gm.	GROSS APPEARANCE	CNS	EYE, EAR	FACE, MOUTH	CARDIO-VASCULAR	LUNG
7	2.8				Cerebral hemisphere / Infundibulum, Rathke's	Lens nearing final shape	Palatal swellings / Dental lamina, Epithel.	Pulmonary vein into left atrium	
8	3.7				Primitive cereb. cortex / Olfactory lobes / Dura and pia mater	Eyelid / Ear canals	Nares plugged / Rathke's pouch detach. / Sublingual gland	A-V bundle / Sinus venosus absorbed into right auricle	Pleuroperitoneal canals close / Bronchioles
10	6.0				Spinal cord histology / Cerebellum	Iris / Ciliary body / Eyelids fuse / Lacrimal glands / Spiral gland different	Lips, Nasal cartilage / Palate		Laryngeal cavity reopened
12	8.8				Cord-cervical & lumbar enlarged, Cauda equina	Retina layered / Eye axis forward / Scala tympani	Tonsillar crypts / Cheeks / Dental papilla	Accessory coats, blood vessels	Elastic fibers
16	14				Corpora quadrigemina / Cerebellum prominent / Myelination begins	Scala vestibuli / Cochlear duct	Palate complete / Enamel and dentine	Cardiac muscle condensed	Segmentation of bronchi complete
20						Inner ear ossified	Ossification of nose		Decrease in mesenchyme / Capillaries penetrate linings of tubules
24		32	800		Typical layers in cerebral cortex / Cauda equina at first sacral level		Nares reopen / Calcification of tooth primordia		Change from cuboidal to flattened epithelium / Alveoli
28		38.5	1100		Cerebral fissures and convolutions	Eyelids reppen / Retinal layers complete / Perceive light			Vascular components adequate for respiration
32		43.5	1600	Accumulation of fat		Auricular cartilage	Taste sense		Number of alveoli still incomplete
36		47.5	2600						
38		50	3200		Cauda equina, at L-3 / Myelination within brain	Lacrimal duct canalized	Rudimentary frontal maxillary sinuses	Closure of: foramen ovale / ductus arteriosus / umbilical vessels / ductus venosus	
First postnatal year +					Continuing organization of axonal networks / Cerebrocortical function, motor coordination / Myelination continues until 2-3 years	Iris pigmented, 5 months / Mastoid air cells / Coordinate vision, 3-5 months / Maximal vision by 5 years	Salivary gland ducts become canalized / Teeth begin to erupt 5-7 months / Relatively rapid growth of mandible and nose	Relative hypertrophy left ventricle	Continue adding new alveoli

FETAL DEVELOPMENT CHART

GUT	UROGENITAL	SKELETAL MUSCLE	SKELETON	SKIN	BLOOD, THYMUS LYMPH	ENDOCRINE
Pancreas, dorsal and ventral fusion	Renal vesicles	Differentiation toward final shape	Cartilaginous models of bones Chondrocranium Tail regression	Mammary gland		Parathyroid assoc-iated with thyroid Sympathetic neuro-blasts invade adrenal
Liver relatively large Intestinal villi	Müllerian ducts fusing Ovary distinguishable	Muscles well represented Movement	Ossification center Sternum	Basal layer	Bone marrow Thymus halves unite Lymphoblasts around the lymph sacs	Thyroid follicles
Gut withdrawal from cord Pancreatic alveoli Anal canal	Renal excretion Bladder sac Müllerian tube into urogenital sinus Vaginal sacs Prostate	Perineal muscles	Joints	Hair follicles Melanocytes	Enucleated R.B.C.'s Thymus yields retic-ulum and corpuscles Thoracic duct Lymph nodes; axillary iliac	Adrenalin Noradrenalin
Gut muscle layers Pancreatic islets Bile	♀ ♂ Seminal vesicle Regression, genital ducts		Tail degenerated Notochord degenerated	Corium, 3 layers Scalp, body hair Sebaceous glands Nails beginning	Blood principally from bone marrow Thymus-medullary and lymphoid	Testicle-Leydig cells Thyroid-colloid in follicle Anterior pituitary acidophilic granules Ovary-prim. follicles
Omentum fusing with transverse colon Mesoduodenum, asc. & desc. colon attach to body wall. Meconium. Gastric, intest. glands	Typical kidney Mesonephros involuting Uterus and vagina	In-utero move-ment can be detected	Distinct bones	Dermal ridges hands Sweat glands Keratinization		Anterior pituitary-basophilic granules
	No further collecting tubules			Venix caseosa Nail plates Mammary budding	Blood formation decreasing in liver	
						Testes-decrease in Leydig cells
						Testes descend
	Urine osmolarity continues to be relatively low			Eccrine sweat Lanugo hair prominent Nails to fingertips		
			Only a few secondary epiphyseal centers ossified in knee		Hemoglobin 17-18gm Leukocytosis	
			Ossification of 2nd epiph. centers-hamate, capitate, proximal humerus, femur New ossif. 2nd epiph. centers till 10-12 yrs. Ossif. of epiphyses till 16-18 yrs.	New hair, gradual loss of lanugo hair	Transient (6 wk) erythroid hypoplasia Hemoglobin 11-12 gm 7S gamma globulin produced by 6 wks. Lymph nodes develop cortex, medulla	Transient estrinization Adrenal-regression of fetal zone Gonadotropin with feminization of ♀ 9-12 yr.(onset); masc. of ♂10-14 yr.(onset)

FETAL DEVELOPMENT CHART

PREFACE

The experience of working as nurses in a university-affiliated facility for several years prompted the development of this reference guide for nurses and other health care professionals.

Because of the large geographic area served by our program, it became apparent that there was a need for more available guidance to the health care professional in identification and assistance of families with children having potential developmental problems.

Our many contacts with community-based nurses have shown they are working with children and families in a variety of settings. Frequently, the community-oriented nurse will refer children suspected of having a developmental problem to a diagnostic clinic such as a university-affiliated facility for an evaluation. She may then become the local coordinator for the implementation of recommendations, monitor or work directly with the child and family on an ongoing basis, and/or may continue to be a liaison between health care agencies.

The nurse often serves as a consultant to other community persons who may desire to refer a child suspected of having developmental problems.

Information in this guide is meant to assist the professional in defining a problem in a more succinct manner. In essence, the general concepts in each chapter serve as a screening mechanism in the context of the specialty of developmental concerns.

ACKNOWLEDGMENTS

Support in part for the development of this guide was made possible by the following grants: Maternal-Child Health Grant Project 926, Bureau of Community Health Services, Department of Health, Education, and Welfare; Colorado State (MCH) Mental Retardation Grant C-291028; and Social Rehabilitation Services Grant 59-P-40129/8-03.

A special appreciation is extended to Opal Every, Harold Martin, Bill Borthick, Ronald Tompkins, and Terry Collins for their support in this endeavor.

CONTRIBUTORS

Kathleen Bryant, M.A., Senior Instructor, Department of Physical Medicine and Rehabilitation, University of Colorado School of Medicine, Denver, Colorado

Elna Cain, R.N., M.S., Child Health Nursing Consultant, Colorado State Health Department, Denver, Colorado

Jane Chapman, R.N., Ph.D., Assistant Clinical Professor of Clinical Psychology, University of Colorado Medical Center; Private Practice, Clinical and Consulting Psychology, Denver, Colorado

William van Doorninck, Ph.D., Psychologist, Associate Professor of Pediatrics, University of Colorado School of Medicine, Denver, Colorado

Marion Downs, M.A., Associate Professor of Otolaryngology (Audiology), University of Colorado School of Medicine, Denver, Colorado

Brian G. Fraser, J.D., Executive Director, National Committee for Prevention of Child Abuse, Chicago, Illinois

Marilyn J. Krajicek, R.N., M.S., Chief Nurse, JFK Child Development Center; Instructor, Department of Pediatrics, School of Medicine; Assistant Clinical Professor, School of Nursing, University of Colorado Medical Center, Denver, Colorado

Annette Lansford, M.D., Practitioner of Developmental Pediatrics, Carle Clinic, Urbana, Illinois; former Director of the High Risk Infant Clinic, Pediatric Outpatient Department, University of Colorado Medical Center, Denver, Colorado

Philomena Lomena, M.S., Chief of Nutrition, JFK Child Development Center, University of Colorado Medical Center, Denver, Colorado

Linda Lord, R.P.T., M.P.H., Chief Physical Therapist, JFK Child Development Center; Instructor, Department of Physical Medicine and Rehabilitation, University of Colorado Medical Center, Denver, Colorado

Marie-Louise Lubs, Ph.D., Assistant Professor of Pediatrics, University of Colorado School of Medicine, Denver, Colorado

Cole Manes, M.D., Ph.D., Associate Professor of Pediatrics, University of Colorado School of Medicine, Denver, Colorado

Paula Roberts, R.N., M.S., Nursing Consultant, Inborn Errors of Metabolism and Child Development, University of Colorado Medical Center, Denver, Colorado

Alice I. Tearney, R.N., M.S., Nursing Consultant, JFK Child Development Center, University of Colorado Medical Center, Denver, Colorado

Cyndi Thero, Consultant/Screening Specialist, Unique Systems Corporation, Englewood, Colorado

Nancy Matthews Weaver, M.S., Educational Consultant, Denver, Colorado

DETECTION OF DEVELOPMENTAL PROBLEMS IN CHILDREN

I
NURSING ASSESSMENTS— SCREENING FOR DEVELOPMENTAL PROBLEMS

A Home Visit— As Related to a Diagnostic Clinic Evaluation

Alice I. Tearney, R.N., M.S. *

The public health nurse is often called upon to assist in the evaluation process when a child and his family are referred for evaluation. She has the distinct advantage of observing a child and family apart from the clinic setting, including the home and the community in which they live. The nurse in the small community or rural area, who has been in the public health position for any length of time, has usually acquired invaluable insight into the local structure of the community and the cultural aspects of the families who reside there. Although it is true that the individual personality of the nurse as helper could be an adverse factor in obtaining a true picture of the home situation, past experience has been for more positive than negative situations. The importance of interpersonal relationships as defined by many authorities is perhaps the top priority ingredient for the nursing home visit. Rogers (1961) feels that effective helping must include positive regard, congruence, and empathetic understanding between patient and helper in order to accomplish a helping situation. The

*Nursing Consultant, John F. Kennedy Child Development Center, University of Colorado Medical Center, 4200 East 9th Avenue, Denver, Colorado 80220.

home visit is an ideal start for a positive helping process. At this time the home setting will assist the helper in beginning to understand concerns or problems from the patient's frame of reference. It is much easier and faster to obtain a gestalt of the problem when one has had the opportunity to be a part of the living situation, even though only for a few hours.

The following material is included as a guide which can be enlarged upon depending on the specific needs of the individual being evaluated.

It is very important that an appointment be confirmed with the family before making the home visit. At this time a request can be made to be certain the patient, as well as well as other family members, is available at this time. These members may include family or persons residing in the home on a fairly permanent basis. The father's presence is requested (if a father is in the home) if he is usually home during the majority of the child's waking hours. (Example: If the father works a 3:00 to 11:00 p.m. shift, it is preferable that he be present for the home visit.)

The following format and information are very helpful data for evaluation purposes.

I. Introduction

This paragraph includes who is being referred and why. If the family is referred by an agency, a statement is now made as to the agency's previous contacts as well as the results of these contacts.

II. Description of the Environment

A. Community

A descriptive paragraph as to the type of community and neighborhood, including upkeep and apparent socioeconomic level, is helpful. An assessment of these factors gives a clue as to the status of the family in a given community.

B. Home

The home is best described in terms of adequacy of furnishings and facilities for activities, such as sleeping, eating, and playing, that are pertinent to the family life style. Toys are to be described rather than stated as "appropriate for the child's age." Provisions for music, reading, and recreation for the entire family are identified.

C. Unusual Features

Sleeping arangements are to be mentioned, particularly if the arrangement indicates such situations as a large child sleeping in a 6-year crib or children sleeping in the parents' bed. The reasons for such arrangements are important.

III. Behavior in the Home

Observation of the child's behavior at home is extremely valuable information when comparing his behavior in the clinic. It is important to describe this behavior in order to support or contradict those behaviors observed in the clinic. Some of these behaviors or states can range from quiet, pleasant, cooperative, and placid, to anxious, manipulative, oppositional, and angry. Situational examples are very helpful in assessing what happens at home.

IV. Interaction

A. Observations of interactions are a crucial part of the home visit. These should be noted in relation to siblings, sibling with parent, and also the manner in which the environment is used by those persons present at the time of the visit. Examples of interactions are: annoyance, tension, restriction other than necessary, safety measures, positive or negative feelings conveyed, praise, discipline used, and intervention and planning (in contrast to a crisis approach).

B. It is helpful to have a short paragraph on each family member who is present. This paragraph essentially includes a physical description of the person and interactional observations during the visit.

   1. If the family member is a younger child, ask him/her to show his bed and toys. Ask about a favorite toy and playmates. It is generally very productive to spend some time individually with each family member.

   2. If the family member is an older child, it is sometimes helpful to elicit concerns he/she has for the sibling being evaluated. Are they aware of the reason for the evaluation?

C. Routine of the Usual Day

   1. Is this given in a spontaneous or restricted manner?

   2. It is usually necessary to supply questions to complete question 1.

   3. The routine is most helpful when it encompasses the entire family. This will give a good picture of family function or functions which will assist in planning for realistic recommendations.

D. Nutrition Screening

This can be accomplished very readily by using a simple 24-hour recall method. If the mother or adult giving the information is inclined to be vague, it is helpful to obtain a sample of a day's menu. This includes the number of servings and approximate size of servings, such as measurement in ounces.

E. Denver Developmental Screening Test (DDST)

This must be done according to the instructional manual. It is useful not only to obtain a picture of the child's function but perhaps more important to compare developmental performance at home with that in a clinic situation. Observational comments on the reverse side of the form are very important data to consider. This situation is an excellent opportunity to screen other children in the home for possible concerns. These concerns might be fairly obvious to a professional and not observed by a parent. Most often the nurse is the only person who has seen the remainder of the family. Knowledge of the total family is essential for realistic intervention.

F. Support System for the Family versus Isolation

1. The presence or absence of peers readily available to a child can be a positive or negative factor when assessing and planning for a family.

2. The local support system available to parents and family as a whole is oftentimes the most convenient vehicle for accomplishing the recommended intervention. These support systems vary considerably with each community and state. The nurse in a small community has a wealth of information about relationships within its confines and can lend invaluable information when planning support for a family.

3. Relatives and friends are sometimes the "significant persons" to the family being helped. It is also true that relatives can work adversely regarding an objective intervention plan. Therefore, a careful look at relationship dynamics is very important before enlisting their assistance. Church contacts and groups within this structure are oftentimes overlooked when they could render valuable assistance in selected cases. A public agency, which is the most obvious choice of assistance for intervention, may also be nonexistent in a small community. There are times when a creative health person has motivated and enlisted a tremendous amount of

assistance through channels at the local high school. Some high school students have been given academic credit for such assistance, providing that the proper instruction and supervision are incorporated into the system.

The preceding suggestions given are but a beginning sample of what possibilities may be present in a truly helping situation.

LITERATURE CITED

Caldwell, B. M., J. Heider, and B. Kaplan. 1966. The Inventory of Home Stimulation. Paper presented at the meeting of the American Psychological Association, September 1966.

Chapman, J., and H. Chapman. 1975. Behavior and Health Care: A Humanistic Helping Process. Mosby, St. Louis.

Rogers, C. 1961. On Becoming a Person. Houghton Mifflin Co., Boston.

I NURSING ASSESSMENTS— SCREENING FOR DEVELOPMENTAL PROBLEMS

B Background Information

Marilyn J. Krajicek, R.N., M.S.*

The following questionnaire has been adapted from the John F. Kennedy Child Development Center Questionnaire, the University of Colorado Medical Center, Denver, Colorado.

MATERNAL INFORMATION

Mother's name _____ Birthdate _____
Address_____
Ethnic background _____ Birthplace_____
Religion_____ Health_____

PREGNANCY HISTORY: Maternal Factors

Any problems in getting pregnant? _____
Date of last menstrual period _____
What month did prenatal care begin?_____
Where?_____

---

*Chief Nurse, John F. Kennedy Child Development Center; Instructor, Department of Pediatrics, School of Medicine; Assistant Clinical Professor, School of Nursing, University of Colorado Medical Center, 4200 East 9th Avenue, Denver, Colorado 80220.

Weight before pregnancy_____Weight gained during pregnancy_____
Medication taken: Vitamins_____ Birth control pills_____ Aspirin_____
                     Other medicines (list) _____

_____

Any medications or narcotic drugs taken before or during the pregnancy __

_____

History of smoking during the pregnancy_____ Have you ever
smoked?_____ How long?_____ Cigarettes per day_____
Were there any illnesses before or during the pregnancy? (describe)_____

History of vaginal bleeding (describe)_____

History of morning sickness (describe) _____

Any swelling of upper or lower extremities or any other parts of the body
(describe)_____
History of elevated blood pressure during pregnancy (describe)_____

Medical problems (describe) _____
History of hospitalizations (describe)_____
Operations (describe) _____
Did any accidents occur during the pregnancy? (describe)_____

Any infections during first trimester (describe) _____
Any x-rays during pregnancy_____ When _____
Describe eating habits during the pregnancy _____

Were there any unusual worries? _____

Describe the baby's movements during pregnancy _____

When did they begin?_____
Any problem getting pregnant with child being referred for evaluation ___
Any history of the following (if so, describe):
    Mentally retarded or neurologically handicapped infant _____

    Premature birth _____
    Repeated miscarriage; dates _____
    Stillbirth _____
    Ectopic pregnancy _____

Abruptio placenta or placenta previa _____

_____

Interuterine growth retardation _____

_____

Blood group incompatibility_____

_____

GENETIC DISORDERS: Family History

If a history of any of the following has occurred (on either side of the family), list the person or persons and relationship to person being interviewed: all serious, chronic or recurrent illnesses or abnormalities, such as birth defects, diabetes, known sterility, allergies, convulsions or epilepsy, mental or emotional disorders, slow development, mental retardation, school problems, cerebral palsy, muscular disorders, cancer, leukemia, thyroid disease, deafness, or blindness.

PATERNAL INFORMATION

Father's name _____   Birthdate _____
Occupation _____   Religion_____
Ethnic background _____   Years of schooling_____
Health _____
Any history of unusual illnesses _____

_____

X-rays in father of child _____
When _____

BIRTH HISTORY

Child's name _____   Birthdate _____
Birthplace_____
Was the baby born on time_____ early_____ late_____
Length of labor _____
Type of anesthesia or pain relief:
   Sedative_____   Shot for pain_____
   Spinal or caudal_____   Other_____
Was mother awake when the baby was born?_____
Type of delivery: Natural_____   Breech_____
                     Cesarean section_____   Forceps_____

Mother's blood group (ABO)_____ Mother's Rh factor_____
Baby's blood group (ABO)_____ Baby's Rh factor_____
Infant's condition at birth _____

Were there any problems during the first week of life (feeding difficulties, etc.)?_____

_____

Baby's birth weight _____
Head circumference_____
Was the child ever hospitalized after birth?
Cause   Where
                        When

_____
_____
_____

DEVELOPMENTAL MILESTONES

Held head erect _____   Stood alone_____
Smiled_____   Walked without holding_____
Rolled over front to back_____   Rode tricycle_____
Rolled over back to front_____   Ran with good control _____
Sat alone _____   Played "pat-a-cake," "peek-a-boo,"
Recognized parents _____   or "bye-bye"_____
Showed fear with strangers_____   Toilet training started_____
Crawled_____   Toilet training finished _____
Said mama or dada _____   Masturbation _____
Said any single words _____   Used two- to three-word phrases___
Drank from cup _____   Used sentences _____
Pulled to standing _____

HEALTH HISTORY

Breast or bottle fed _____   Did child eat well?_____
Childhood diseases (list age and anything unusual about any of them)
Mumps _____   3-day or German measles_____
Chicken pox _____   7-day or red measles_____
Roseola _____   Scarlet fever _____
Whooping cough_____

Immunizations (dates or ages received; any unusual reaction):
DPT series _____   Smallpox _____
DPT booster _____   Measles _____
Polio (oral) _____   Polio (shots) _____
Rabies_____   Other _____

Dental history:
Has child ever been examined by a dentist?_____
When was child's last visit to the dentist? _____

If child has had any of the following, please indicate and explain details:
Accidents_____
_____
Operations _____
_____
High fever, unknown cause_____
Pneumonia _____
Anemia _____
Urine infection or disease _____
Constipation _____
Vision problems _____
Crossed eyes _____
Speech problems _____
Hearing problems _____
Frequent ear infections_____
Foot problems (any special shoes, braces, etc.) _____
Skin disease or abnormality _____
Allergies _____
Birthmarks _____
Seizures or convulsions _____
Unusual fears _____
Sleeping difficulties _____
Head banging _____
Breath holding_____
Temper tantrums _____
Discipline problems_____
Ingestion of toxins or poisons such as drugs, cleaners, etc._____
Other illnesses _____

CHILD AND FAMILY INTERACTIONS IN ENVIRONMENT

List members living in household and relationship if any to child: _____
_____

Describe what the child is like _____

_____

How does the child get along with siblings, baby sitters?_____

_____

What things does the child like to do?_____

_____

Describe the toys and play activities the child enjoys_____

_____

Has the child been separated from his/her family? (At what age, duration, and reason for separation) _____

_____

SCHOOL INVOLVEMENT

1. Has child ever been in preschool classes? If so, when and where

_____

_____

2. Has child ever been in special education? If so, when, where and what kind

_____

_____

3. Has child ever been in remedial classes? If so, when, where, and by whom

_____

_____

4. Has child ever been in special tutoring? If so, when, where, and by whom

_____

_____

5. Has child ever received speech therapy? If so, when and where _____

_____

6. Has child ever received any other type of therapy? _____

7. List schools (with dates) that child has attended:

_____

_____

_____

_____

HEALTH CARE LIST

Doctor who delivered child

Name _____

Address _____

City and state _____

Hospital where child was born

Name _____

Address _____

City and state _____

Places where child has received
care:include hospitals,
agencies (welfare, visiting
or public health nurse service, child development center,
and other outpatient services)

Name _____

Address _____

City and state _____

Name _____

Address _____

City and state _____

Name _____

Address _____

City and state _____

Name _____

Address _____

City and state _____

Name _____

Address _____

City and state _____

Name _____

Address _____

City and state _____

Physicians who have cared
for child

Name _____

Address _____

City and state _____

Name _____

Address _____

City and state _____

Name _____

Address _____

City and state _____

Signature _____

Relationship _____

Date _____

I
NURSING ASSESSMENTS— SCREENING FOR DEVELOPMENTAL PROBLEMS

ℂ Physical Examination of the Child

Elna Cain, R.N., M.S. *

Child health service involves assessment and intervention. Assessment, or accumulation of data, includes history (the most important), physical examination, and results of screening tests.

The nurse's right and responsibility to examine a child are no longer in question. Nurses providing direct care to children make numerous judgments, such as whether the child is sick or healthy, whether there are indications of need for further evaluation or care by other health professionals, and what types of nursing intervention are indicated. Nurses are expected to give guidance and counseling to parents regarding how to keep children healthy; how to manage acute, chronic, and emergency health problems; and how to promote maximum development of children physically, mentally, socially, and emotionally. In order to initiate nursing intervention, make accurate judgments, make appropriate referrals, and provide effective counseling, nurses must gather and utilize all available data.

All nurses have at some time done physical examinations of patients. Some have examined an individual completely; more have examined par-

* Child Health Nursing Consultant, Colorado Department of Health, 4210 East 11th Avenue, Denver, Colorado 80220.

ticular parts. It is common practice in hospitals for nurses to "observe" or examine the affected part, for example, the abdomen for bleeding, swelling, distention, etc., after abdominal surgery; the foot for circulation, bleeding, movement, etc., after leg surgery; the head, ears, eyes, reflexes, mental state, response to sensory stimuli, and vital signs after head injury. In spite of some rather sophisticated observations expected in certain circumstances, there has been less emphasis on nurses doing systematic complete examinations.

The way to learn to do a physical examination is to practice. Skills are sharpened through experience. All nurses have a great deal of information and experience to draw upon, although much of it is tucked away and needs to be stimulated to return to consciousness.

TECHNIQUES

The techniques of physical examination are:

> *inspection*—looking at, observing; *palpation*—feeling lightly or firmly, probing and pressing; *percussion*—tapping, striking, either directly or indirectly (indirectly includes striking finger held on body with percussion hammer or finger of other hand); *auscultation*—listening, usually with a stethoscope.

TOOLS

The nurse's most basic and important tools for a physical examination are the hands, eyes, ears, and other senses. They are all that is necessary for gathering a large quantity and wide range of valuable information. There are a number of other items which are useful and helpful to add when resources are available and as the nurse's skills are refined. Tools and equipment desirable are itemized at the end of each part of the physical examination outline along with techniques used for examination of each body part or system.

USE OF THE PHYSICAL EXAMINATION OUTLINE

The following outline is designed for the beginning examiner (or as a refresher for an experienced one). It includes listing of normal findings in children; findings within the range of normal (which can be a wide and sometimes confusing range); and some "not present" specifics, that is, things to check as not being present, aimed at ensuring absence of deformity, syndromes, and relatively obscure disease conditions. Although the body areas are listed in the order in which they are most often recorded, examination may not proceed in the exact order of the outline. Thoroughness, thoughtfulness, and a systematic examination are the most important considerations. Confidence, based on sophistication in decision making, depth of knowledge, and evolution of skills, increases with study, practice, and periodic verification of the nurse's findings.

If some of the examing tools are not available, some of the techniques seem too complicated, or the things to check too numerous, items can be completed when the time is right. Simply looking at (*inspecting*) and feeling (*palpating*) an entire child yield a wealth of useful and valid data to combine with historical data for decision making (see Figure 1).

APPROACHES AND SUGGESTED EXAMINATION SEQUENCES

To gain maximum cooperation from an infant or child, it is best to start by establishing a pleasant relationship with the parent, then to seek to establish a relationship with the child by talking, using a toy, or doing a screening procedure such as the Denver Developmental Screening Test. Save upsetting procedures until last. Before starting the examination, wash your hands in warm water. Establish a routine for infants and for older children which is followed consistently. Include all body areas in the routine. Allow for some flexibility to fit the responses of each child.

It is usually easiest to examine an infant of up to about 6 to 9 months of age on a padded table. Older infants and children of up to 3 or 3½ years of age are usually best examined while sitting on the parent's lap. Older children can sit alone on a chair or table. All need to lie down for examination of the abdomen and genitalia (and infants must be supine to check for congenital dislocated hip).

The following is one suggested routine or sequence of examination for infants and for older children. (The child must be undressed, but it is not necessary to do it all at once. Have the parent or child do the undressing.)

Infants

Examine top-to-bottom front, then top-to-bottom back. Have undressed except for diaper. Place baby face up on table → *head* (except eyes, nose, mouth, throat, ears) → *face* → *head* and *neck nodes* → *neck* → *clavicles* → *arms* (including axillary nodes) → *hands* → *chest* (including listening to heart and anterior lungs) → *abdomen* → *legs* → *feet* → Remove diaper. *inguinal area* → *genitalia* → *anus* → For *dislocated hip* → Leave diaper on table. Turn baby on his/her stomach, matching diaper area to diaper. → *back of head* → *neck* → *spine* → *back of chest* (including listening) → *buttocks* →

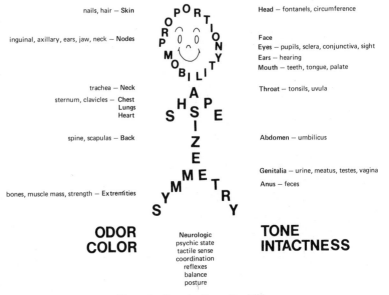

Figure 1. Examination of a child.

back of legs → Turn face up. Replace diaper. → *neurological tests* (not already included) → *eyes* → *nose* → *mouth* → *throat* → *ears*.

Older Children

Examine top, front, and back, then bottom, front, and back. Have undressed from waist up. → *head* → *face* (except eyes, nose, mouth, throat, ears) → *head* and *neck nodes* → *neck* → *clavicles* → *arms* → *hands* → *chest* (including listening front and back) → Replace shirt, blouse, or dress. Have clothes from waist down removed except underpants. → *legs* → *feet* → Have child lie down on table. → *abdomen* → Pull underpants down. →*genitalia* → *anus* → Replace underpants. → Have child walk for observation of gait, touch toes, and do standing *neurological tests* → *eyes* → *nose* → *mouth*→ *throat* → *ears*.

PHYSICAL EXAMINATION OUTLINE

I. Measurements
- A. Temperature.
- B. Pulse.
- C. Respirations.
- D. Blood pressure.
- E. Height or length.
- F. Weight.
- G. Head circumference.

   Record height, weight, and head circumference percentile for age or graph on standardized form.

   Instrumentation: thermometer, blood pressure apparatus with child-size cuffs, scales, tape measure, measuring board.

II. General Appearance
- A. Alert.
- B. Active.
- C. Well nourished.
- D. Healthy appearing.
- E. Strong voice quality (or cry).
- F. No striking physical features.
- G. Warm, close mother-child relationship.
- H. Readily responsive to examiner.

   Describe activity and appearance of child as observed during contact and examination.

   Technique: *inspection.*

III. Skin
- A. Warm.
- B. Color consistent with racial background.
- C. No cyanosis or jaundice.
- D. Hematocrit (or hemoglobin) within normal limits. (Anemia cannot be determined by skin color.)
- E. Good turgor. (Skin is elastic and returns readily to normal position after pinching.)
- F. No lesions, bruises, abrasions, or rashes.
- G. No birthmarks.

   Skin is examined on each part of the body as other examinations are made of that part. Hair and nails are part of the skin. Techniques: *inspection, palpation,* including use of hematocrit, centrifuge, or hemoglobinometer.

IV. Lymph nodes

   Nonred, nontender and cool nodes to 3 mm diameter may be

normal; to 1 cm in cervical and inguinal areas, usually normal. Specific sites to check are included throughout outline.

Techniques: *inspection, palpation.*

V. Head

    A. Symmetrical. (May be asymmetrical in early weeks of life.)

    B. Fontanels closed. (Posterior closed by 2 months, anterior by 18 months. If open, fontanels should not be bulging or sunken when infant sitting.)

    C. No suture ridges felt. (Ridges may be felt to 6 months.)

    D. Hair evenly distributed without bald or worn spots or unusually low forehead or neck hairline.

    E. Hair (*what*) color, of soft, silky texture with sheen.

    F. Scalp clear of lesions, scaling, or foreign bodies.

    G. Occipital lymph nodes not enlarged.

Techniques: *inspection, palpation* primarily. May add *percussion* and *auscultation* (see Alexander and Brown, 1974; Barness, 1972; Chinn and Leitch, 1973; Committee on Standards of Child Health Care, 1972; Silver, Kempe, and Bruyn, 1973).

VI. Face

    A. Generally

        1. Well proportioned.

        2. Symmetrical at rest and in movement.

        3. Features similar to those of parents.

        Technique: *inspection.*

    B. Eyes

        1. (*What*) colored irises.

        2. Pupils equal in size, round in shape.

        3. Pupils constrict and dilate in response to light, bright and dim.

        4. Pupils clear.

        5. Light reflection falls on same area of both pupils.

        6. Eyes move together. (Muscle imbalance may be normal for 6 months but follow closely.)

        7. Eye covered when other eye fixed on object does not move when cover removed (cover test).

        8. Follows object side-to-side, up and down and obliquely. (By 4 months most babies can follow 180° side-to-side.)

        9. Eyes converge when object brought close to nose.

       10. Red reflex observed. (Light shown through pupil at close range reflects red glow similar to the yellow reflection from a cat's eyes.)

11. Eyes not sunken.
12. No circles under eyes.
13. Sclerae and conjunctivae clear.
14. Lids level.
15. No epicanthic folds. (Inner lid folds normal in children of Mongolian race.)
16. Eyes not unusually widely or closely set.
17. Vision 20/(20, 30, 70, etc.), 20/(20, 30, 70, etc.).
    Technique: *inspection* including use of light and vision screening equipment. Use of ophthalmoscope may be learned from references and/or a person with skill in its use.

C. Ears
    1. External ears well shaped and symmetrical.
    2. Symmetrically placed and set so that part of each ear falls above an imaginary line drawn from outer corner of eye to occiput.
    3. Ear canals open.
    4. Tympanic membranes pearly gray with light reflex, umbo, long process, and short process of malleus visible. (See Figure 2.)
    5. Hearing screening passed. (Audiometer screening for older children; bell, whisper, or other screening tech-

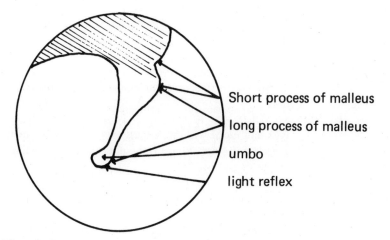

Short process of malleus

long process of malleus

umbo

light reflex

Figure 2. Tympanic membrane of right ear. (Drawn by Ronald Tompkins, John F. Kennedy Center.)

niques, together with history and language development, may be used for younger children.)
6. Lymph nodes behind ears not enlarged.
    Techniques: *inspection,* including use of otoscope and hearing screening equipment; *palpation*.

D. Nose
    1. Patent bilaterally.
    2. No nasal drainage or crusting.
    3. Septum midline.
    4. Mucosa pink and firm.
    5. Bridge of nose not unusually flat or broad.
    6. No pain or tenderness on pressure over sinuses.
        Techniques: *inspection,* including use of light; *palpation.*

E. Mouth
    1. Mucous membrane pink, moist, and without lesions or redness.
    2. Tongue proportionate to mouth, symmetrical at rest and in movement, extends to gum margins.
    3. Gums clear.
    4. Palate intact and not unusually high or narrow.
    5. (*number of*) teeth have no dental caries. (Estimate of average number of teeth is obtained by subtracting 6 from age in months up to 20 primary teeth. Refer if no teeth by 12 months.)
    6. No malocclusion, overlapping, or unusual spacing of teeth noted.
    7. No drooling noted (after 2 years).
    8. Lymph nodes under jaw not enlarged.
        Techniques: *inspection,* including use of light; *palpation.*

F. Throat
    1   Pink and moist with no redness, pus, or drainage noted.
    2. Tonsils not obstructing airway, not touching in midline, no pus or crypts.
    3. Uvula midline and single.
    4. No consistent mouth breathing.
    5. Gag reflex present.
        Technique: *inspection,* using light and tongue blade.

VII. Neck
    A. Mobile, symmetrical.
    B. No pain evident when neck flexed chin to chest.

C. Not webbed or unusually short. (Babies have short necks.)
D. Trachea midline.
E. Thyroid not palpable.
F. Sternocleidomastoid muscles symmetrical with no swelling or masses.
G. Anterior and posterior neck lymph nodes not enlarged.
   Techniques: *inspection, palpation.*

VIII. Chest
    A. Generally
        1. Symmetrical and not unusually shaped at rest and with movement.
        2. Clavicles at same level and smooth.
        3. Sternum not sunken or protruding.
        4. No beading on ribs.
        5. Breasts flat with nipples symmetrical. (There should be no breast engorgement or development from 1 month of age to puberty.)
        6. Axillary lymph nodes not enlarged.
        Techniques: *inspection, palpation.*

    B. Lungs
        1. Respirations regular at rate of (*number*) per minute (some irregularity is normal).
        2. Chest expands equally with breathing.
        3. Breath sounds clear and equal on both sides anteriorly and posteriorly.
        4. No rales (fine crackles on inspiration), friction rub (coarse or grating sound), or wheezes (musical sounds on inspiration or expiration) heard.
        5. Skin test negative for tuberculosis.
        Techniques: *inspection, palpation, auscultation,* including use of stethoscope, tuberculin skin test.

    C. Heart
        1. Pulse rate (*number*) per minute, regular and full.
        2. Heart sounds clear with regular rhythm; rate slightly faster on inspiration than expiration. (There are two parts of the normal heart sound, commonly called lub-dub or S_1 and S_2. Either may normally be heard as a "split" sound in children, especially "dub" or S_2. Extra sounds, blowing or whispering sounds, or unusual rhythm indicate need for referral, although in many cases the unusual sounds may be normal and not indicate heart pathology.)

Techniques: *inspection, palpation, auscultation,* including use of stethoscope.

Items covered are adequate for beginning examination of the chest. Increased skill and additional points to check can be gained by study of references and/or the assistance of a preceptor. *Percussion,* a useful method in chest examination, may be added in the same manner.

IX. Abdomen
- A. Symmetrical, protruding. (Children's abdomens may normally protrude until puberty.)
- B Firm muscle tone.
- C. Umbilicus not protruding, no umbilical hernia.
- D. Bowel sounds present every 20 seconds. (Heard as metallic short tinkling, they are normally heard every 10 to 30 seconds. Should listen to bowel sounds before deep palpation.)
- E. Abdomen nontender on light or deep palpation or when pressure quickly withdrawn.
- F. Liver palpable 1 cm below costal margin. (Not always palpable. Best felt on inspiration. May be normally palpable up to 2 cm below right lower rib throughout childhood.)
- G. Spleen not palpable. (Rarely palpable up to 2 cm below left lower rib. Should be soft and nontender.)
- H. No masses felt on superficial or deep palpation.
- I. Inguinal lymph nodes not enlarged.
- J. Femoral pulses felt equally bilaterally.

  Techniques: *inspection, palpation, auscultation,* including use of stethoscope.

  As for the chest, increased skill and additional points to check may be gained by study and/or use of a preceptor. *Percussion* may be added in the same manner.

X. Genitalia
- A. Urinary stream strong and wide.
- B. Urine clear yellow.
- C. Urine negative on dip stick screening.
- D. Male
  1. Testes in scrotum. (Examine gently, placing pressure in inguinal area on side being palpated with other hand. Left testicle is normally lower than right. Testes are not consistently found in scrotum but presence of both at some time should be determined.)

    2. Meatus at tip of penis and not inflamed.

    3. No inguinal hernia or hydrocele noted.

    4. No loose or constricting foreskin (if circumcised).

    5. Foreskin not constricting (if not circumcised). (Foreskin usually becomes easily retractable by 4 years. Do not forceably retract foreskin.)

E. Female

    1. Meatus and vaginal opening visible.

    2. No discharge from vagina (until near puberty).

    3. Clitoris small.

    4. Labia symmetrical, not adherent or enlarged.
Techniques: *inspection, palpation*, with use of urine dipsticks.

XI. Anus

A. No irritation, fissures, or tags.

B. Stool soft and formed (if observed).
Techniques: *inspection, palpation;* rectal examination may be added with the assistance of a preceptor or study of references.

XII. Extremities

A. Mobile with full range of joint movement possible actively and passively.

B. Of equal length, strength, muscle mass, mobility, and temperature.

C. Muscle tone firm.

D. Long bones straight.

E. Feet mobile. (Feet turning in, out, down, or up usually within normal limits until child has been walking 1 to 2 years if they can be passively overcorrected.)

F. Legs straight. (Bowed legs usually normal to 2½ years, flat feet to 3½ years, knock-knees from 2 to 3½ years.)

G. Walks easily and fluidly with good balance. (Broad-based gait normal to 3 years.)

H. Inguinal, gluteal, and thigh folds symmetrical. (Asymmetry may be normal, but is an alert to examine carefully for signs of dislocated hip.)

I. Legs abduct equally when knees and hips are flexed in frog position. No click felt or heard. (See Figure 3.)

J. No instability noted in hips.

K. All digits present and proportionate, not clubbed.

L. Hands symmetrical with no simian line. (Single line extending across palm.)

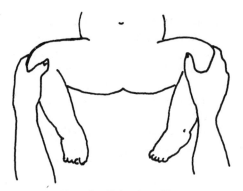

Figure 3. Abduction of legs.

M. Nails intact, firm, and flexible.
Techniques: *inspection, palpation.*

XIII. Back
A. Spine straight and mobile.
B. Vertebral processes palpable.
C. No indentations or tufts of hair noted over spine. (Pilonidal dimple near the sacrum is common but should be checked carefully to see that there is no opening or sinus and that skin is not irritated.)
D. Back symmetrical.
E. Scapulas at an equal level when standing (or lying in infant) and when child bends over to touch toes (in older child).
F. Iliac crests at an equal level.
G. No tenderness noted on pressure or percussion over kidneys.
Techniques: *inspection, palpation, percussion.*

XIV. Neurological
A. Infants
1. Developmental landmarks reached for age. (As measured or observation on screening test such as Denver Developmental Screening Test or a developmental scale.)
2. Behavior, activity, and degree of alertness appear appropriate for age.
3. Posture, balance, and coordination appropriate for age.
4. Cry lusty.
5. Infant responsive to cuddling.
6. Deep tendon reflexes present and symmetrical. (The most commonly tested are the patellar, by striking just

below knee; Achilles, by striking just above heel with foot pushed up; biceps, by striking thumb against lower point of insertion while child's arm is flexed; and triceps, by striking just above bent elbow. In each case, expected response is contraction of muscle which has tendon stimulated. Strike briskly with side of hand, tip of finger, or percussion hammer.)

7. Babinski reflex positive. (Up to 18 months the abnormal or positive response of toe fanning and great toe moving up is observed when foot is stroked from lateral part of heel up lateral part of foot and across below toes.)

8. Hand grasp equal. (Reflex grasp strongest between 1 and 2 months.)

9. Tonic neck reflex noted. (Leg and arm extend on side to which head is turned, flex on opposite side. Reflex lasts up to 5 months.)

10. Moro reflex present. (Startle response with extension then flexion of extremities with arms grasping as around an object. Lasts up to 5 months.)

11. Landau reflex present. (Back straight or arched diver fashion when baby suspended over table prone, one of examiner's hands supporting abdomen, other on back. Lasts from 3 to 18 months.)

B. Older child

1. Developmental landmarks reached for age (as measured or observed by comparing with developmental screening test or scale, plus historical information regarding learning achievements).

2. Behavior, activity, and degree of alertness and cooperation appear appropriate for age.

3. Balance steady with eyes open and closed. (Tested by such activities as standing, walking, standing with both feet together, on one foot with eyes open and closed, and walking heel-to-toe forward and backward with eyes open.)

4. Fine and gross motor coordination appropriate for age. (Tested by such activities as manipulation of toys, drawing, alternatively striking palms of examiner with one hand at a time, touching examiner's finger held before face then own nose alternately, touching own nose with eyes closed, hopping, skipping, jumping rope.)

5. Demonstrates ability to spell, do math problems, reason and do abstract thinking. (Tested by such activities as asking child to verbally spell two or three words and do some simple math problems mentally, asking to explain a nursery rhyme, familiar story, or proverb.)
6. Demonstrates appropriate short and long term memory for age. (As tested by such things as asking to repeat a series of numbers; remember a word or phrase during exam; recite alphabet, rhyme, pledge to flag; give address, birthdate, etc.)
7. Deep tendon reflexes present and asymmetrical.
8. Babinski reflex negative.
9. Senses of touch, taste, smell intact.

    Responses to neurological tests, ability to perform various activities, and quality of responses depend on child's age and individual rate of development. Although there is a wide range of normal, referral to references and developmental norms plus experience lead to increasing ability to distinguish normal from abnormal responses. Many indicators of neurological function are included in the examination of individual body parts. The examiner should incorporate into the examination routine neurological tests representative of the various areas of neurological function, such as balance, fine and gross motor ability, coordination, reflexes, and memory.

    Techniques: *inspection* including toys, *percussion* including percussion hammer.

The following are some suggestions for making maximum use of the outline and other references.

1. Write highlights of the outline on an index card to refer to during practice.
2. Practice examining as many children as possible. Include children of various ages as well as two or more children of the same age.
3. Compare historical data with physical findings.
4. Pursue any unusual finding by seeking additional history and focusing more attention on examination of possibly related areas.
5. At first, write down all findings in the manner in which they appear in the outline. Although this is time consuming, it leads to rapid learning of many points to check in relation to all body parts.

6. Think about each normal finding in relation to corresponding possible abnormalities. Use references as necessary.

7. Periodically study references, looking for more things to check, relationships between physical findings, answers to questions that come to mind during practice.

CONCLUSION

A nurse's role is to distinguish normal from abnormal, then to decide whether intervention is indicated. If intervention is indicated, the nurse determines what type and the degree of urgency. Judgments become easier and more reliable as skills in examination are more fully developed. Confidence is the most important and rewarding outcome for the nurse who learns to do a systematic physical examination.

LITERATURE CITED

Alexander, M., and M. S. Brown. 1974. Pediatric Physical Diagnosis for Nurses. McGraw-Hill Book Co., New York.

Barness, A. 1972. Manual of Pediatric Physical Diagnosis. 4th Ed. Yearbook Medical Publishers, Chicago.

Chinn, L., and C. J. Leitch. 1973. Handbook for Nursing Assessment of the Child. University of Utah Printing Service.

Committee on Standards of Child Health Care. 1972. Standards of Child Health Care. 2nd Ed. American Academy of Pediatrics, Evanston, Ill.

Silver, H. K., C. H. Kempe, and H. B. Bruyn. 1973. Handbook of Pediatrics. Lange Medical Publishers, Los Altos, Calif.

I
NURSING ASSESSMENTS— SCREENING FOR DEVELOPMENTAL PROBLEMS

D Use of Screening Tools

Paula Roberts, R.N., M.S. *

Many social, economic, educational, and political forces have caused the nurse and society to look critically at nursing knowledge and skills. The "assessment" tools nurses are learning and employing are no longer geared extensively to acute illness, but are increasingly utilized to promote health, well being, and the development of optimum abilities in the individual. A dynamic example is knowledge about normal growth and development, and appropriate application of this knowledge (i.e., anticipatory guidance) to enhance the child's rate of development, as well as the pleasure the family gains from involvement in and promotion of this evolving process. Because of the basic premise that all people have a right to quality medical and nursing care and resultant health services a number of delivery systems have developed, most notably Medicaid with its Early and Periodic Screening, Diagnosis and Treatment (EPSDT) Program. The mandate is out for early recognition and prevention of disease and/or disabling conditions and maintenance of health with accompanying appropriate intervention as needed. This intervention is most timely when begun before signs and

---

*Nursing Consultant, Inborn Errors of Metabolism, and Child Development, University of Colorado Medical Center, 4200 East 9th Avenue, Denver, Colorado 80220.

symptoms of disease become manifest and, hopefully, given before serious damage occurs. The tools available to the nurse for this are varied and numerous. Recognizing this fact, the author will elaborate later on in this chapter on the screening tool she is most familiar with: The Denver Developmental Screening Test (DDST), developed in Denver at the University of Colorado Medical Center.

DEFINITION OF TERMS

To begin a discussion of use of screening tools, one must first define some terms so that the reader and the author have a similar reference base.

Screening as accepted by the World Health Organization Regional Committee for Europe is "the presumptive identification of unrecognized disease or defects by the application of tests, examinations, or other procedures which can be applied rapidly. Screening tests sort out apparently well persons who probably do not have a disease from those who probably do have the disease. A screening test is not intended to be diagnostic. Persons with positive or suspicious findings must be referred to their physicians for diagnosis and necessary treatment" (Wilson and Lungner, 1968). There are four types of screening that may be employed: *mass screening, selective* or *prescriptive screening, multiple screening,* and *multiphasic screening.* An entire population may be screened by *mass screening* techniques, e.g., newborn screen for phenylketonuria. On the other hand, *selective* or *prescriptive screening* can be applied to a given group of people at higher risk than the general population for a condition, e.g., Jewish people for Tay-Sachs. *Multiple screening* is often used in the schools to evaluate the hearing and vision of school children, thus ruling out two potential problem areas at one time. *Multiphasic screening*, on the other hand, extends the number of screening measures used on a given individual from the two or three used in multiple screening to a battery of as many as 10, as might be employed on a well child visit, as is recommended by Medicaid in their EPSDT program. There are other factors about screening that are also pertinent. Screening measures may be used to periodically follow an individual or group, monitoring their present state of well being, e.g., periodic urinalyses; this is a screening factor called *surveillance.* In addition, screening tools have some degree of *sensitivity* (accuracy in correctly differentiating an individual with a disease from the general population) and *specificity* (accuracy in correctly differentiating the individual without the disease from those having it). Some screening tools are *standardized,* meaning compared with a standard (i.e., development) (Frankenburg, 1973).

SCREENING SELECTION

In deciding to become involved in a screening program the nurse has a number of issues to consider: his or her skills with a given screening tool, the population to be screened, the cost, the time factor for the nurse, the patient, and the family, where the screening will be done, and where or to whom positive findings will be referred, to mention only a few. With these issues in mind, the nurse may wish to carefully select which conditions are to be screened.

The criteria (Frankenburg, 1973) for disease selection for screening include the following.

1. Is the disease or condition serious or potentially so?
2. Are there diagnostic tests and procedures available to follow-up on a positive screening result identifying the diseased individual from the borderline or nondiseased individual?
3. Will the prognosis be altered in the condition if identified before symptoms appear?
4. Is the disease or condition being screened for treatable or controllable?
5. Is there an adequate time interval between that when the condition can be picked up by a screening tool and the optimum time for treatment?
6. Is the condition being screened for relatively prevalent?
7. Are there facilities for referral of positive screening findings?
8. What is the cost for the entire process of screening, with early identification, diagnosis, and treatment versus late identification, diagnosis, and treatment?

With the above factors in mind, the type of screening test the nurse uses is important. The *criteria* that should be used in selection of a screening tool are the following (Frankenburg, 1973).

1. Is the screening tool acceptable to the patient, the family, and the nurse?
2. Is the tool *reliable* (are screening results consistent each time the tool is used)?
3. Is the tool *valid* (does it measure what it is supposed to measure)?
4. Is the total cost reasonable?

THE DENVER DEVELOPMENTAL SCREENING TEST

With the above introduction to screening in hand, the author will now look at the nurse's use of one standardized screening tool for "assessing" development in preschool children, the Denver Developmental Screening

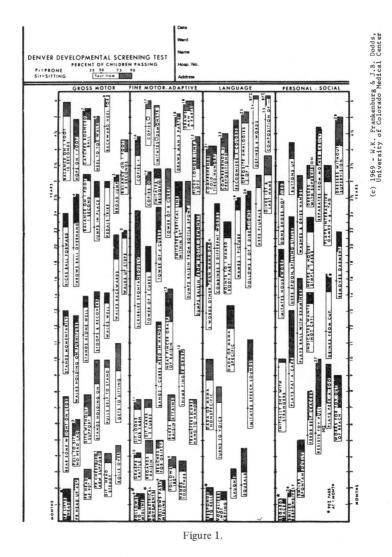

Figure 1.

Test (Figure 1). A significant characteristic of this screening tool is that it was carefully *standardized* on over 1,000 normal preschool children in the Denver metropolitan area. This factor alone increases confidence in the stability of this tool, for it was thus possible to develop normative data on when mastery of certain developmental tasks occurs on a large number of children from varying socioeconomic backgrounds. The DDST also offers

Key to DDST.

1. Try to get child to smile by smiling, talking or waving to him. Do not touch him.
2. When child is playing with toy, pull it away from him. Pass if he resists.
3. Child does not have to be able to tie shoes or button in the back.
4. Move yarn slowly in an arc from one side to the other, about 6" above child's face. Pass if eyes follow 90° to midline. (Past midline; 180°)
5. Pass if child grasps rattle when it is touched to the backs or tips of fingers.
6. Pass if child continues to look where yarn disappeared or tries to see where it went. Yarn should be dropped quickly from sight from tester's hand without arm movement.
7. Pass if child picks up raisin with any part of thumb and a finger.
8. Pass if child picks up raisin with the ends of thumb and index finger using an over hand approach.

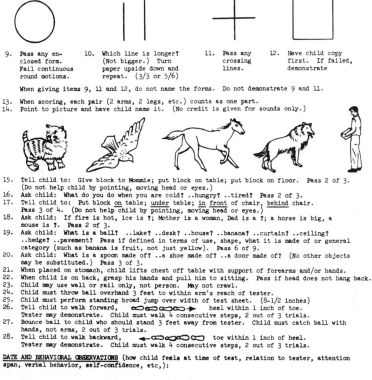

9. Pass any en-closed form. Fail continuous round motions.
10. Which line is longer? (Not bigger.) Turn paper upside down and repeat. (3/3 or 5/6)
11. Pass any crossing lines.
12. Have child copy first. If failed, demonstrate

When giving items 9, 11 and 12, do not name the forms. Do not demonstrate 9 and 11.

13. When scoring, each pair (2 arms, 2 legs, etc.) counts as one part.
14. Point to picture and have child name it. (No credit is given for sounds only.)

15. Tell child to: Give block to Mommie; put block on table; put block on floor. Pass 2 of 3. (Do not help child by pointing, moving head or eyes.)
16. Ask child: What do you do when you are cold? ..hungry? ..tired? Pass 2 of 3.
17. Tell child to: Put block on table; under table; in front of chair, behind chair. Pass 3 of 4. (Do not help child by pointing, moving head or eyes.)
18. Ask child: If fire is hot, ice is ?; Mother is a woman, Dad is a ?; a horse is big, a mouse is ?. Pass 2 of 3.
19. Ask child: What is a ball? ..lake? ..desk? ..house? ..banana? ..curtain? ..ceiling? ..hedge? ..pavement? Pass if defined in terms of use, shape, what it is made of or general category (such as banana is fruit, not just yellow). Pass 6 of 9.
20. Ask child: What is a spoon made of? ..a shoe made of? ..a door made of? (No other objects may be substituted.) Pass 3 of 3.
21. When placed on stomach, child lifts chest off table with support of forearms and/or hands.
22. When child is on back, grasp his hands and pull him to sitting. Pass if head does not hang back.
23. Child may use wall or rail only, not person. May not crawl.
24. Child must throw ball overhand 3 feet to within arm's reach of tester.
25. Child must perform standing broad jump over width of test sheet. (8-1/2 inches)
26. Tell child to walk forward, ⬭⬭⬭➔ heel within 1 inch of toe. Tester may demonstrate. Child must walk 4 consecutive steps, 2 out of 3 trials.
27. Bounce ball to child who should stand 3 feet away from tester. Child must catch ball with hands, not arms, 2 out of 3 trials.
28. Tell child to walk backward, ◄⬭⬭⬭ toe within 1 inch of heel. Tester may demonstrate. Child must walk 4 consecutive steps, 2 out of 3 trials.

DATE AND BEHAVIORAL OBSERVATIONS (how child feels at time of test, relation to tester, attention span, verbal behavior, self-confidence, etc,):

Figure 1. Denver Developmental Screening Test. See text for explanation of test items.

an exciting, concise, easy to administer (15 to 20 minutes when the tester is proficient), systematic approach to "assessing" development in pre-school children. It establishes the idea of a range of normality for ac-complishing developmental milestones. It encourages a broader look at the preschool child in the areas of *personal-social* skills (relating to people and independence), *fine motor-adaptive* skills (hand-eye coordination, problem solving, and perception), *language* skills (hearing, use of the spoken word, and interpretation of the spoken word), and, lastly, *gross motor* skills (posturing, locomotion, and coordination) (Frankenburg et al., 1973).

Emphasis has been placed on the fact that the DDST aids the nurse in *assessing* preschool development . . . and it does *just* that. It does not measure the developmental level of a child, nor tell the level at which the child being examined functions. (To do this one needs to administer a *diagnostic* developmental exam, such as the Bayley Scales of Infant Development, the Revised Yale Developmental Schedules, the Gesell Developmental Schedules, or the Cattell Infant Intelligence Scale.) What the DDST is designed to do is tell the screener how the child he is screening compares with other children of his age (the standardization population), that is, is his development, as assessed by the DDST, age appropriate (*normal*) or is it not so, being *questionable* or *abnormal*, or perhaps even *untestable*. To carry this a step further, if upon a second screening the child continues to fall in the *questionable, abnormal*, or *untestable* screening result category, then follow-up is indicated, for the DDST is not diagnostic and thus does not explain the reason behind the deficit in the child's performance.

It is natural for a nurse working with children and families to wish to see the child do well on developmental screening, but it is not in the best interests of the child to let this feeling rule the testing situation. (If there really is a problem the sooner it is identified and referred the sooner the child and family will benefit from appropriate intervention.) The DDST affords the nurse an opportunity to *objectively* assess development of a child, which points out how essential it is that the nurse administer each test item as carefully described in the manual (Frankenburg et al., 1973).

Since there is a very specific way of administering the test items in the DDST, the author identifies some common errors of administration often made:

1. In the *personal-social* sector:
   a. "Feeds self cracker" . . . a task to see whether the child is being allowed to do self-feeding, not one to determine whether a child puts things in his mouth (a means of environmental exploration for an infant);
   b. "plays 'pat-a-cake' " . . . a task to see whether the child plays games of a simple nature, not one to determine whether a child can clap his hands (a midline task that is examined in the *fine motor-adaptive* sector);
   c. "plays ball with examiner" . . . looks at whether the child will

interact with the examiner, not whether the child can roll a ball (a *fine motor-adaptive* skill);

d. "resists toy pull" ... a task to see whether the child has the ego development to resist the examiner taking the toy away from him so that he deliberately pulls back on the toy, not one to be confused with the grasp reflex of an infant (a *fine motor-adaptive* skill);

e. "buttons up" ... looks at self-help skills in dressing and its accomplishment determines whether a child "dresses with or without supervision," both tasks requiring the ability to button up;

f. "separates from mother easily" ... looks at the child's ego strengths for separating from his mother to being with a babysitter who is not a family member, thus buffering the separation situation;

g. "drinks from cup" ... a reportable item, like many others in this sector, must be administered carefully, keeping your questions as open ended as possible, and being sure to follow up on the mother's answer (in this instance to determine that there is no spout on the cup and that the child is holding it himself and spilling very little).

2. In the *fine motor-adaptive* sector:

a. "scribbles spontaneously" ... is a reportable item that you may have answered as *no opportunity* ... however, since you are looking at a *fine motor-adaptive* ability you may wish to give the child the opportunity to scribble spontaneously, thus being able to note the *quality* of his performance;

b. "dumps raisin from bottle—spontaneously" ... must be administered before "dumps raisin from bottle—demonstration" in order to allow the child to problem solve on his own (this also applies to "copies square" versus "imitates square demonstration" in order to allow the child to demonstrate a higher level perceptual skill copying versus copying a demonstrated figure);

c. "tower of 2, 4, 8 cubes" or "draws man three parts or six parts" ... are other examples of gradation of skills where if the child cannot do "tower of 2 cubes" or "draws man three parts" then it follows he does not pass "towers 4 or 8 cubes" or "draws man six parts" and vice versa; if he can accomplish the more difficult tasks he automatically passes the simpler tasks (emphasizing how developmental skills build on one another);

d. "neat pincer" ... a task often difficult to differentiate from "thumb finger" is best identified by watching the position of the child's wrist and elbow in addition to his fingers.

3. In the *language* sector:

   a. "opposite analogies two of three" . . . the child need only pass two of the three samples and most children readily understand temperature and size differentiation before six;

   b. "defines words/six of nine" . . . a task that causes many nurses to object to the words *hedge* and *pavement* because they are uncommon; however, there are seven other words for the child to define, of which he need only define six correctly.

4. In the *gross motor* sector:

   a. "bears some weight on legs" . . . is one item one does not want to see much before 3 months of age, for this may be stiffness in the baby if occurring early (a sign of spasticity);

   b. "walks up steps" . . . many items in this sector are reportable, thereby eliminating the opportunity to observe these skills; therefore, in administration, it is essential that one ask questions as open endedly as possible, as in this test item where one wants to know the neuromuscular ability of the child . . . thus asking "how does your child get up steps" will allow the mother or caretaker to *describe* the child's behavior without a stated expectation, as would be the case if stated "Does your child walk up steps?"

A word now about *scoring* the DDST. The scoring opportunities open to the examiner are "pass" (P), "Fail" (F), "refusal" (R), or "no opportunity" (N.O.). There tends to be some confusion about what a "fail" means in relation to the overall test interpretation. A test item that is failed does not become a concern unless it is located left of the age line, meaning that 90 percent of children *younger* than the child being screened are able to do the item . . . this constitutes a "delay." One delay in and of itself does not mean a problem for the child. Unfortunately, many examiners have jumped to the conclusion that a child is not developmentally age adequate (normal) because the child fails some test items. It should be remembered that the child is not expected to pass all of the test items, and that a test has not been completely administered until there are at least three failures in each sector (along with three passes in each sector) and all test items intersected by the age line have been administered.

Now for the author's biases in test administration and interpretation: 1) try to elicit all the behavior one can from the child, so the screener can observe the *quality* of performance, and be sure to make note of it on the back of the test form under "behavioral observations"; 2) administer this screening tool with the mother or caretaker present, so that the screener can observe and record the mother-child interaction; 3) remember to tell the mother that the child will be requested to do a number of test items above his ability (have him fail) and that the screener does not expect him to pass all of the test items administered to him.

A word of caution is indicated. This screening tool has been carefully standardized on over 1,000 preschool children to establish the norms for each developmental task. Thus, in order for the test to mean anything (be both valid and reliable) the screener must administer and score each test item as it is carefully explained in the manual. The exact test materials in the kit must be used and, if substitution of a broken or missing item is necessary, it *must* be exactly like the item, particularly in size and shape. If the screener does not adhere to this then the test results will not be comparable with the standardized population results and, thus, not valid (Frankenburg et al., 1973).

Please note that it is critical when planning to screen children for any difficulty that a good referral system be established. The nurse using the DDST must, therefore, be certain to have medical back-up for "delays" that are identified. The DDST is not diagnostic; thus a thorough medical examination and psychological evaluation are critical in getting the appropriate intervention to the child and family. Although it is recommended that the parents be referred to the physician for interpretation of the test results, it is recognized that, with the educational background of the nurse, appropriate interpretation and counseling leading to referral when necessary may be expected (Frankenburg et al., 1973).

In conclusion, in analyzing the DDST in relation to the World Health Organization definition for screening, it becomes apparent that this screening tool meets the criteria of being administered easily, is not diagnostic, and is reliable and valid. It can be used for surveillance of development in a child, allowing for periodic rescreening. It has a high degree of sensitivity and specificity if administered correctly. The DDST is also an acceptable screening tool to the child, the family, and the nurse, while the cost factor is minimal.

Other preschool screening tools developed, standardized, and employed at the University of Colorado Medical Center which have demonstrated good reliability and validity, easy administration, are inexpensive to purchase and employ, and fun for the child are listed in Table 1 and described below (Krajicek and Roberts, 1976).

The Denver Eye Screening Test (DEST) looks at children from six months and older with regard to visual acuity and non-straight eyes. If

Table 1. Screening tools

Test	Ages used	Description
Denver Developmental Screening Test (DDST)[a]	1 month–6 years	Individually administered developmental screening test; not diagnostic[b]
Denver Eye Screening Test (DEST)[a]	6 months and older	Individually administered vision screening test; not diagnostic[c]
Denver Articulation Screening Exam (DASE)[a]	2½ years–7 years	Individually administered articulation screening test; not diagnostic
Denver Audiometric Screening Test (DAST)[a]	3 years and older	Individually administered hearing screening test; not diagnostic[d]
Pediatric Developmental Questionnaire (PDQ)[a]	1 month–6 years	Parent administered and used as "prescreening" tool for developmental screening[e]

[a]Distributed by LADOCA, Project and Publishing Foundation, Inc., East 51st Avenue & Lincoln Street, Denver, Colorado 80216 [(303) 222-3605].
[b]Identifies child with I.Q. below 70.
[c]Identifies child with visual acuity and nonstraight eyes problems.
[d]Identifies child with serious hearing loss below 25 decibels.
[e]Gets parent's perspective of the child developmentally.

employed properly it is able to identify those children with amblyopia (impaired vision in one eye), refractive error, and strabismus (crossed eyes) from the general preschool population as to normal, abnormal, or untestable performance. Screening time when proficient is 5 to 10 minutes.

The Denver Articulation Screening Exam (DASE) looks at children from two and one-half years to seven years, screening their ability to reproduce 30 sounds intelligibly (clearness in general conversation). It is limited to looking at articulation problems, not more general speech and language skills (i.e., vocabulary, language ability). If employed properly it is able to identify those children with articulation problems which are not appropriate for age, when compared with the standardization population as to normal or abnormal performance. Screening time when proficient is approximately 5 minutes.

The Denver Audiometric Screening Test (DAST) looks at children from three years and older, screening for serious hearing loss (25 dB or less). Using puretone audiometry it can identify children in the preschool years, as compared with the standardization population, in regard to normal, abnormal, or untestable performance. Screening time when proficient is approximately 5 to 10 minutes.

A new "pre-screening" tool, the Pre-screening Developmental Questionnaire (PDQ), has recently become available. It is presented to the parent or guardian of the child, requesting they answer ten age-appropriate developmental questions regarding their child's abilities, indicating "yes" or "no" for each task questioned. The nurse and/or other professionals can note any "no" responses and follow up with some developmental screening tool.

A slide tape presentation "Introduction to Pediatric Screening," Reference #S-2885, is available from: Sales Branch, National Audio-Visual Center, Washington, D.C. 20409. This presentation further emphasizes and clarifies the rationale for employing pediatric screening.

SUMMARY

Thus, screening has been defined and criteria for selecting conditions to be screened and selecting a screening tool have been described. In addition, standardizing screening tools such as the Denver Developmental Screening Test (DDST), Denver Eye Screening Test (DEST), Denver Articulation Screening Exam (DASE), the Denver Audiometric Screening Test (DAST), and Pre-screening Developmental Questionnaire (PDQ) have been presented. All of these screening tools can assist the nurse and other professionals to identify problems early, to maximize intervention in maintaining and promoting health and well being, and to promote the development of optimal abilities in the individual. Additional assessment tools and tests are listed in Table 2 (Krajicek and Roberts, 1976).

Table 2. Screening tools and tests

Test	Ages	Description
1. Behavioral Developmental Profile (Marshalltown)	0–6 years	Designed to measure development of handicapped and deprived children. For individualized programming of preschool children within the home setting. The profile is divided into three scales which include: communication, motor, and social. The profile is used in conjunction with the behavioral prescription guides which are available.
2. Neonatal Behavioral Assessment Scale (Brazleton)	First few days of life	Behavioral assessment scale and psychological scale for the newborn human infant. Graded scales of procedures are used which include an evaluation of control over interfering motor activity on the part of the infant response to animate and inanimate stimulation. Stimulation assessment of the neurological adequacy and estimates of the attentional excitement exhibited by the infant. The scale should be accompanied by a pediatric and neurological examination. Estimated time for administration: 30 minutes.
3. The Washington Guide to Promoting Development in the Young Child	1–52 months	Provides for assistance in systematically observing the child in the areas of motor feeding, sleep, play, language, discipline, toileting, dressing. Expected tasks are presented, as well as suggested activities to provide for enhancement of growth and development.
4. Alpern-Boll	Birth to preadolescence	Provides for a reliable screening of a child's development in the areas of physical, self-help, social, academic, and communication (20 to 40 minutes to administer).
5. Individual Learning Disabilities Classroom Screening Instrument	Grades 1, 2, 3	Designed to aid classroom teachers in a systematic identification of children who have difficulty learning academic material.

#	Instrument	Age Range	Description
6.	McCarthy Scales of Children's Abilities	2½ to 8½ years	Assesses motor and cognitive behaviors in the areas of verbal perceptual performance, quantitative, general cognitive, memory, and motor. For children from various ethnic, regional, and socioeconomic groups.
7.	Cooperative Preschool Inventory	2 to 6½ years	Assessment of achievement in areas of concept, activation-sensory; activation-numerical; personal-social responsiveness; and associative vocabulary. Limited norms are provided on performance of children 2 to 6½ years identified as those of lower and middle class background (standardized).
8.	Caldwell Home Inventory	Birth to 3 years	Home observation for measurement of the environment assessing of areas which include: 1) emotional and verbal responsivity of mother; 2) avoidance of restriction and punishment; 3) organization of environment; 4) provision of appropriate play materials; 5) maternal involvement with the child; 6) opportunities for variety in daily routine.
9.	Caldwell Home Inventory	3 to 6 years	Home observations for measurement of the environment including the following: 1) provision of stimulation through equipment, toys, and experiences; 2) stimulation of mature behavior; 3) provision of a stimulating physical and language environment; 4) avoidance of restriction and punishment; 5) pride, affection, and thoughtfulness; 6) masculine stimulations; 7) independence from parental control.
10.	The Boyd Development Progress Scale	Birth to 8 years	Measures three areas of function which include: motor skills (fine and gross motor activities), communication skills (cover comprehension or cognitive skills which measure what the child can do by actual testing), and self-sufficiency, which measures through interviewing of the parent what the child typically does.
11.	A Developmental Approach	Birth to early infancy	Focuses on the vulnerable child, the evolution of basic neurological patterns and the maturation of the central nervous system.

LITERATURE CITED

Frankenburg, W. K. 1973. Pediatric screening. *In* I. Schulman, Advances in Pediatrics. Vol. 20. Yearbook Medical Publishers, Inc., Chicago.

Frankenburg, W. K., J. B. Dodds, and A. W. Fandal. 1973. Denver Developmental Screening Test Manual/Workbook for Nursing and Paramedical Personnel. University of Colorado Medical Center, Denver.

Krajicek, M. J., and P. Roberts. 1976. Nursing. *In* R. Johnston and P. Magrab (eds.), Developmental Disabilities: Evaluation, Treatment, and Education. University Park Press, Baltimore.

Wilson, J. M. G., and C. Lungner. 1968. Principles and Practice of Screening for Disease. WHO Publ. Health Papers 34: 1.

SUGGESTED READINGS

Frankenburg, W. K. 1970. Evaluation of screening tests and procedures. Proceedings on Earlier Recognition of Handicapping Conditions in Childhood. University of California School of Public Health.

Frankenburg, W. K. 1970. Development and developmental screening. Current Pediatric Diagnosis and Treatment, pp. 28–35.

Frankenburg, W. K. 1971. Developmental screening of preschool aged children. Current Issues in Mental Retardation and Human Development, pp. 29–44. President's Committee on Mental Retardation, Washington, D. C.

Frankenburg, W. K. 1973. Increasing the lead time for the preschool aged handicapped child. *In* Not All Little Wagons Are Red: The Exceptional Child's Early Years, pp. 24–33. The Council for Exceptional Children, Arlington, Va.

Frankenburg, W. K. 1973. Developmental screening in infants and children. *In* Brennemann's Practice of Pediatrics, Harper & Row, Publishers, Inc., New York.

Frankenburg, W. K. 1974. Development and developmental screening. Current Pediatric Diagnosis and Treatment, pp. 27–36.

Frankenburg, W. K., and B. W. Camp. 1975. Pediatric Screening Tests. Charles C Thomas, Publisher, Springfield, Ill.

Frankenburg, W. K., B. W. Camp, J. A. DeMersseman, and S. F. Voorhees. 1971. The Reliability and Stability of the Denver Developmental Screening Test. Child Devel. 42: 1315.

Frankenburg, W. K., B. W. Camp, and P. A. VanNatta. 1971. Validity of the Denver Developmental Screening Test. Child Devel. 42: 475.

Frankenburg, W. K., and M. E. Cohrs. 1973. Acceptance of home screening: How to reach the unreached. Clin. Res. 21(2).

Frankenburg, W. K., and N. P. Dick. 1973. Development of preschool aged children: Racial-ethnic and social class comparison. Clin. Res. 21(2).

Frankenburg, W. K., and J. B. Dodds. 1967. The Denver Developmental Screening Test. J. Pediat. 71–181.

Frankenburg, W. K., and A. D. Goldstein. 1971. Procedure for Selecting Screening Technicians. University of Colorado Press, Denver.

Frankenburg, W. K., A. Goldstein, and B. W. Camp. 1971. The revised Denver Developmental Screening Test: Its accuracy as a screening instrument. J. Pediat. 79: 988.

Frankenburg, W. K., A. Goldstein, A. Chabot, B. W. Camp, and M. Fitch. 1970. Training the indigenous nonprofessional: The screening technician. J. Pediat. 77: 564.

ADDRESSES FOR PROCUREMENT
OF ADDITIONAL SCREENING TOOLS/TESTS

Department of Special Education
  Marshall—Poweshiek Joint County School System
  9 Westwood Drive
  Marshalltown, Iowa 50158

Developmental Profile (Alpern-Boll)
  Psychological Development Publications
  7150 Lakeside Drive
  Indianapolis, Indiana 46273

Preschool Inventory
  Educational Testing Service
  1947 Center Street
  Berkeley, California 94704

Individual Learning Disabilities
  Classroom Screening Instrument
  Learning Pathways, Inc.
  Evergreen, Colorado 80439

McCarthy Scales of Children's Abilities
  The Psychological Corp.
  304 East 45th Street
  New York, New York 10017

Caldwell Home Observation for Measurement of the Environment
  (Birth to Three; Three to Six)
  Center for Early Development and Education
  University of Arkansas
  814 Sherman
  Little Rock, Arkansas 72202

Neonatal Behavioral Assessment Scale
  Spastics International Medical Publications
  in Association with William Heinemann
  Medical Books, London
  Philadelphia, Pennsylvania, J. B. Lippincott Company

The Boyd Developmental Progress Scale
   Inland Counties Regional Center, Inc.
   P. O. Box 6127
   San Bernardino, California 92408

A Developmental Approach to Casefinding
   U.S. Department of Health, Education and Welfare
   Public Health Service
   Health Services and Mental Health Administration
   Public Health Service Publication No. 2017–1969
   Superintendent of Documents
   U.S. Government Printing Office
   Washington, D. C. 20402

The Washington Guide to Promoting Development In the Young Child
   Teaching Children with Developmental Problems: A Family Care
   Approach by K. Bernard and M. Erickson
   C. V. Mosby Co., St. Louis, Missouri

III
THE EMBRYONIC PATIENT: AN OPPORTUNITY FOR THE PREVENTION OF DEVELOPMENTAL PROBLEMS

Cole Manes, M.D. *

THE RATIONALE FOR
PRECONCEPTUAL SCREENING AND INTERVENTION

The relevance of embryology to child health lies in the area of preventive rather than remedial medicine. An appreciation of early human embryonic development leads not only to sheer fascination at the precision and intricacy of the developmental processes that are unfolding, but also to an awareness of as yet unexploited opportunities for contributing to the child's safe passage through this critical period. Most of us have had the saddening experience of treating newborns with severe defects that almost certainly could have been prevented, and the frustrating experience of realizing in retrospect that timely and informed management of the pregnancy might have accomplished far more than our attempted "cures." It should be one of the goals of children's medicine to identify the causes of these defects and to use all possible resources to prevent them. The purpose of this chapter will be to review briefly the events of human embryonic development and to indicate what the health professional can do, even at our present incomplete level of understanding, to contribute to the health of the developing child.

The limits to a child's developmental potential are determined by his genetic endowment, which in turn is determined by the genetic material of

---

*Associate Professor of Pediatrics, University of Colorado School of Medicine, 4200 East Ninth Avenue, Denver, Colorado 80220.

the two parental gametes which unite at the moment of fertilization. Common sense as well as scientific evidence lead us to expect that the status of the genetic material of the two gametes can be influenced by the previous history of the parents. The genetic material of the egg and sperm is not immune to harmful environmental influences, and some of these influences—such as irradiation and certain metals and drugs—can even now be identified and eliminated.

However, the outcome of a pregnancy is obviously not determined solely by the genetic status of the fertilized egg. The environment in which the child develops, first as an embryo, later as a recognizably human fetus, and finally into postnatal life, will determine to what extent the genetic potential will be realized. The health status of the mother is therefore of particular importance in creating the optimal environment for the developing child during pregnancy. Because of the rapidity and complexity of embryonic development during the first few days and weeks of pregnancy, the health of the mother during this early period must be assigned an especially high priority. Unfortunately, under our present definition of "prenatal care," the health professional rarely has the opportunity to intervene for the welfare of the child during this extremely critical early period of pregnancy. Expanding our definition of "prenatal care" to include not only these first weeks of pregnancy but even the preconceptual period will require a re-education of the general public and the health profession alike. The potential rewards, in terms of healthier children, should be well worth the effort.

HUMAN EMBRYONIC DEVELOPMENT

Preceding the preface of this book is a chart depicting the progression of anatomical events which characterize human embryonic and fetal development. It must be emphasized that the *age* of the embryo referred to in the chart is timed from the moment of egg fertilization, and not from the last normal menstrual period or an estimate of the time of the first missed period. Egg fertilization occurs shortly after ovulation, and since ovulation itself occurs almost exactly 14 days before the onset of a menstrual period, the time of ovulation can be estimated within a day or two in women with regular menstrual cycles. It should also be pointed out that by the time a pregnant woman has "missed a period" the embryo is almost 3 weeks old.

The chart indicates that very many important things are happening in the embryo even during the first few days and weeks. During this time the fertilized egg must undergo repeated cell division: the embryo must *grow*.

The resulting cells must begin the elaborate process of "differentiation," and, in fact, the cells of the embryo begin to become different from each other after the first 2 or 3 days. Some of these first cells to differentiate will function solely to enable the embryo to implant in the wall of the uterus on the 7th day of pregnancy. These are "trophoblast" cells which contribute to the formation of the placenta and which will produce the hormone chorionic gonadotropin, the presence of which in the blood or urine of the mother is diagnostic of pregnancy.

The cells which will become the embryo itself are initially a rather nondescript clump inside the hollow ball of trophoblast cells. Shortly after the end of this 1st week, however, at about the time the trophoblast cells are making intimate contact with the uterine lining, events of crucial importance to the future child are detectable within this clump of cells. A single body axis is formed, providing the child with a definite anterior-posterior and right-left orientation for all future development. The three standard "germ layers" of the embryo—the ectoderm, endoderm, and mesoderm—are also becoming differentiated from each other and assuming their proper relationships with each other, a prerequisite for all subsequent organ and tissue formation.

Perhaps most dramatically, the basic components of the central nervous system and the circulatory system are assembled by the end of the 4th week. The nervous system begins as a flat plate of thickened ecto-dermal cells along the top of the embryo. This plate rolls up at its lateral edges and the edges fuse with each other as they meet in the midline, forming a "neural tube." The fusion of the edges, hence the closure of the neural tube, begins early in the 4th week of life at a point almost midway along the anterior-posterior embryonic axis, then proceeds toward each end. It is generally completed by the end of the 4th week. Failure of the neural tube to close at all is apparently incompatible with embryonic or fetal survival. However, failure of the tube to complete its closure at one or both ends is generally compatible at least with intrauterine survival. We see these unfortunate infants at birth as anencephalic children (failure of closure at the anterior end) or as children with various degrees of rachischisis or meningomyelocele (failure of closure at the posterior end). Such defects in neural tube closure, although they may reveal an under-lying genetic "predisposition," are almost certainly caused by environ-mental influences.

The heart begins as a pair of tubular structures that form in the anterior mesoderm of the embryo during the 3rd week. These paired heart tubes fuse into a single chamber by about the 22nd or 23rd day of life, at which time the heart begins to beat. The formation of the important septa within this chamber, which divide the single tube into the definitive four-chambered heart, is completed by about the 7th or 8th week of life.

Further inspection of the chart of embryonic development reveals that other things are happening also during the first few weeks. The eye, the ear, the palate, the limbs, the lungs, and the kidneys all begin to assume their definitive locations and shapes in the growing embryo. By the end of the 12th week, in fact, one might be justified in concluding that almost all of the really "important" events which convert the fertilized egg into a recognizable human being have already occurred. The 2nd and 3rd trimesters of pregnancy are mostly periods of growth, of applying the "finishing touches" to the basic structures formed during the 1st trimester. An important exception is the development of the central nervous system, and particularly the brain. The growth and finer differentiation of this system, leading to the behavioral and intellectual capacities which are uniquely human, continue on into the postnatal period.

One important concept that has emerged from studies of embryonic development is that of "critical stages." This concept began with the observation that development proceeds at a characteristic rate; observable events, such as the closure of the neural tube or the formation of fingers, normally occur at quite predictable times. It was then discovered that, if anything interferes with these events, they will *not* occur at a later time. Closure of the neural tube, for example, during the 3rd and 4th weeks of life is a "now or never" event. If it is prevented from closing at that time, it will not close subsequently. Conversely, if it *does* close on schedule, almost nothing that occurs later on will cause it to reopen. The "critical stage" in the formation of any organ may be a period of only a few days, and the environmental agents which are known to harm embryos—drugs, irradiation, viruses—cause the maximum damage to a given organ only if they are present during this brief period. They may cause minimum damage, or no damage at all, if they are present at other times. Critical stages vary from one organ to another. Rubella virus infection, for example, may damage the developing heart during the 4th week of pregnancy. During the 6th week, both the heart and the lens of the eye may be affected, while during the 10th week it is primarily the inner ear which is damaged.

The contrast between the few days which are required for normal neural tube closure (to use this example again), and the lifetime of disability which results from its failure to close properly, should provide a powerful stimulus to the application of preventive medicine in the very early weeks of human life.

OPPORTUNITIES FOR INTERVENTION

As we have already recognized, the opportunities for intervention are generally rare. Most pregnancies "just happen" without much planning, and the pregnant mother is frequently seen by the health professional for the main purpose of confirming her pregnancy after she has missed one or two menstrual periods. It is very unusual to be consulted by prospective parents who are aware of the importance of the early part of pregnancy to the future health of their child and are concerned that pregnancy be initiated under optimum conditions. To create such an awareness and a concern and to increase the opportunities for intervention as indicated will require a sizeable educational effort. The National Foundation/March of Dimes is currently involved in such an effort, and we may hope that the effort will succeed. As health professionals, we may also advise school boards to incorporate such subjects into a curriculum designed for the early high school years. We may also take advantage of every opportunity presented to increase the public awareness by counseling teenagers in the importance of "planned parenthood" or by taking a few minutes to discuss the subject with couples who come for the routine premarital blood test.

If we should be fortunate enough to be involved in such family planning, what can we, at the present time, accomplish in terms of screening and intervention? What can we do to *anticipate* the "high risk infant," and what steps can be taken to lessen the risk? The following outline is only one suggested procedure. As our understanding of the causes of faulty embryonic development increases, this outline will, it is hoped, rapidly expand.

Screening for Familial Disorders

A history of hereditary disorders in either parent's family is obviously of considerable importance, and this subject will be discussed at some length in chapter III. The mode of inheritance of many of these disorders is known (as dominant or recessive, X-linked or autosomal, etc.), and prospective parents can be advised as to the probable genetic risks to their own offspring.

Appraisal of the Medical Status of Both Prospective Parents

Most of this appraisal can be accomplished by taking a history. The presence of endocrine problems or of chronic infectious or metabolic disease is generally recognized by the parents, although the history may elicit suspicious elements which must then be confirmed by the appropriate diagnostic tests.

Endocrine Status   Certain endocrine problems may interfere with the fertility of a couple, but the problems of concern here are those which may be detrimental to the normal development of the embryo and fetus. It is thus the endocrine status of the mother which requires the most careful evaluation.

Thyroid, parathyroid, adrenal, and pancreatic dysfunction in the prospective mother should be recognized and be under the best possible medical control at the time of pregnancy. None of these disorders, if properly controlled, poses any contraindication to pregnancy or threat to the embryo. If the mother is unaware of such problems, but the history discloses suggestive symptoms—such as weight loss, heat intolerance, hair loss, tremor, polyuria, muscle cramps, kidney stones, or changes in skin pigmentation—then she should have the benefit of a complete medical evaluation before pregnancy is attempted.

Infectious Disease   Active syphilis or tuberculosis should obviously be recognized and treated. A susceptibility to rubella virus infection, as determined by antibody titer, should also be tested for (if it has not been done as part of routine premarital testing), so that immunization can be accomplished before pregnancy.

Genital *Mycoplasma* infection, as detected by cervical smear, has been linked to recurrent spontaneous abortion and to congenital defects. This laboratory test may become routinely available and should be used if possible. Prospective mothers should also be advised against eating raw or undercooked meat, because of the possibility of acquiring *Toxoplasma* infection during pregnancy.

Appraisal of the Environmental Status of the Prospective Parents

The interview should attempt to elicit a history of chronic or habitual exposure to environmental agents which could be a threat to the embryo. Although we are again primarily concerned with the prospective mother, we cannot totally ignore the father. Spermiogenesis is a continuous process in males, and agents which are known to be carcinogenic or mutagenic can introduce genetic errors into the rapidly dividing cells of the male gonad. No studies have been carried out to substantiate these risks, but inquiries into the husband's occupational situation may provide information of value to future epidemiologists. It is not too far-fetched to suspect, for example, that prospective fathers who are garage mechanics, painters, agricultural workers (exposed to insecticides and herbicides), plastics workers, or who are employed in the nuclear power plants of the future may incur an increased risk of producing genetically abnormal sperm.

Nutritional Status and Habits Of all the nongenetic factors which are known to contribute to poor embryonic and fetal development, the most important is poor nutritional status in the mother. Poor nutrition may be enforced for socioeconomic reasons or may be voluntary for cosmetic reasons. If the nutritional level is too low, it may well inhibit fertility. Some women are poorly nourished out of mere habit, tending to subsist primarily on "junk foods." These are often teenagers who are either rebelling against parental controls or who simply do not know better. Recent work with laboratory animals has underscored the importance of nutrition during early pregnancy. It has been shown quite clearly that dietary restriction of the trace element zinc, for example, can cause detectable abnormalities in developing embryos within as short a period as 2 to 3 days. Thus, at present, nutritional counseling of the prospective mother is probably the single most important thing the health professional can do to improve the outcome of a pregnancy.

Drug Exposure At the moment, *no* drug can be considered completely harmless to the developing embryo. Drugs which are harmless to adults can be quite toxic to embryos. Even drugs which are harmless to the embryos of other mammals cannot be necessarily assumed to be harmless to human embryos. The most recent and tragic example of this situation was encountered with the drug Thalidomide, which was found completely harmless to rat embryos but obviously caused extensive damage to humans.

It is easy to recognize as "drugs" those chemical compounds which are prescribed for medical reasons. Many women, however, do not consider "over the counter" items, such as diet pills, sleeping medications, nasal decongestants, or aspirin-containing compounds, as "drugs." Still less do they recognize cigarettes, Coke, coffee, artificial sweeteners, dry cleaning materials, or insecticides as "drugs." A history of the habitual use of psychogenic drugs may not be volunteered, or may well be denied, unless its importance to the forthcoming pregnancy is sufficiently stressed.

The best advice to the prospective mother at this moment is: *no drugs whatsoever during pregnancy*. If they must be taken for medical reasons, including excessive nausea during early pregnancy, they should be taken only under supervision of a physician with the intent of keeping the dosage as low as possible.

Other Environmental Exposures We have traditionally cautioned potentially pregnant women against exposure to x-rays. Most radiology units make every effort to schedule routine examinations only during the week following a normal menstrual period. Women in whom pregnancy is established should be counseled to avoid periods of hypoglycemia or prolonged periods at high altitudes. In the list of "things to avoid when pregnant" we should probably also include the excessive use of raw vegetables and plant materials. These foods are unlikely to be a serious source of trouble in humans, although malformed offspring in farm animals have been clearly associated with the ingestion of certain weeds. The tendency which some pregnant human mothers display towards bizarre dietary cravings (green mangoes and vinegar, for example!) might, in unusual or extreme circumstances, pose a threat to the developing child.

The Timing of Conception

Although definite proof in human subjects is lacking, studies with laboratory animals indicate that both egg and sperm undergo "aging" after their release from the gonad. In animals, the union of aged sperm with a normal egg, or an aged egg with normal sperm, can lead to chromosome abnormalities in the resulting embryo. There is, in humans, a definite increase in the incidence of spontaneous abortions in women whose pregnancies followed coitus occurring 2 or 3 days before or after the time of ovulation. Thus, our preconceptual counseling of prospective parents should include a word as to the importance of timing ovulation during the menstrual cycle, using basal body temperature charts or any other reasonably reliable method, and subsequently using this information to attempt conception as close to the time of ovulation as possible.

Reassurance

Perhaps we should end this chapter on a positive note. After enumerating all the things that can go wrong during pregnancy, it is sometimes well to remember that things usually go *right*. The aim of our counseling should not be to create exaggerated anxiety in the prospective parents, but simply to help them recognize certain potential hazards for their future child and to take steps to avoid or correct these situations in a common sense sort of way.

SUGGESTED READINGS

Langman, J. 1975. Medical Embryology. The Williams & Wilkins Co., Baltimore.

Manes, C. 1975. Genetic and biochemical activities in pre-implantation embryos. *In* C. Markert and J. Papaconstantinou (eds.), The Developmental Biology of Reproduction, pp. 133–163. Academic Press, New York.

Saxen, L., and Rapola, J. 1969. Congenital Defects. Holt, Rinehart and Winston, Inc., New York.

IIII GENETIC DISORDERS

Marie-Louise Lubs, Ph.D. *

At least 11 million Americans suffer from a genetic disorder. Almost 3 million of those have genetic forms of mental retardation, 1 million have congenital bone or muscle disorders, more than 1 million have handicaps involving hearing or vision, and 6 million have other specific organ defects. The genetic origin of the defects is varied. There can be extra or missing chromosomal material, either in the form of a whole chromosome or a part of a chromosome, or the defect can be explained by a single mutant gene or by many genes, sometimes in conjunction with environmental factors such as viruses or drugs.

Since the error in the genetic constitution is present in every cell of an individual with a genetic disorder, a correction of the error itself cannot be accomplished and only in a few disorders can the symptoms of the disease be eliminated or lessened. Examples of such methods of treatment are eye glasses, hearing aids, altered diets, and drugs such as insulin. The treatments do not generally accomplish a permanent change; the patient must continue the treatment for the rest of his life. In only a few disorders has surgery provided a cure of the problem so that the patient can resume a normal life. In view of the serious prognosis of so many of the genetically determined diseases, different methods of preventing the birth of affected individuals are becoming increasingly utilized.

In the following sections, the different types of inheritance will be explained and some examples of disorders in each category will be discussed.

THE CHROMOSOMES

Chromosomes consist of very tightly coiled strands of DNA, which is the genetic material. One can compare a chromosome with a string of beads, in which each bead is a gene. Every cell in the human body (except egg and sperm cells) has 46 chromosomes. By treating the cells with different chemicals and stains, it is possible to visualize the chromosomes through a

*Assistant Professor of Pediatrics, University of Colorado Medical School, 4200 East 9th Avenue, Denver, Colorado 80220.

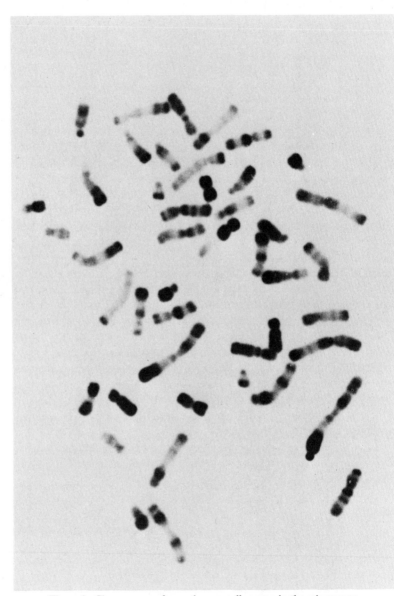

Figure 1. Chromosomes from a human cell as seen in the microscope.

light microscope. Figure 1 is a photograph taken through a microscope. In Figure 2 the chromosomes have been arranged according to length. Twenty-two of the chromosomes have an identical-looking partner or "homologue." One of the members in each of the pairs is derived from the mother and the other from the father of the individual. These 22 pairs are called the autosomes. The 23rd pair is the sex chromosome pair. In women, this pair consists of two identical large chromosomes looking like the letter X and, therefore, named X chromosomes. They are shown in the lower right corner of Figure 2. Males, however, have a different sex chromosome constitution, which is shown in Figure 3. One member of the pair is an X chromosome, as in females. The other is a small asymmetrical chromosome called the Y chromosome.The Y chromosome has to be present for the individual to have functional male reproductive organs.

In the formation of egg and sperm cells, a reduction division takes place, so that only one member of each pair will make up the chromosomal constitution of these cells. Eggs and sperms, therefore, have only 23 chromosomes. All eggs have an X chromosome, half of the sperm cells contain an X, and the other half a Y chromosome. At fertilization, the egg and sperm fuse, making a zygote with 46 chromosomes which will develop

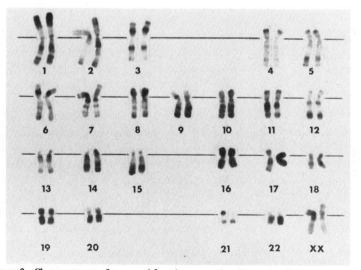

Figure 2. Chromosomes of a normal female conventionally arranged according to total length.

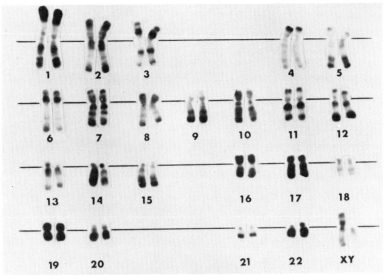

Figure 3. Chromosomes of a normal male.

into the embryo. If the sperm cell contained an X it will be a female fetus, if it contained a Y it will be a male. This is shown schematically in Figure 4.

It is not unusual that something goes wrong in the reduction division so that, instead of having only one member of each pair make up the constitution of the egg or sperm cell, there will be either both homologues or none. This is called a nondisjunction. This abnormal egg or sperm cell will form a zygote that is either missing one chromosome, making a total of 45, or has an extra chromosome, a total of 47 chromosomes. All daughter cells from such a zygote will have the same chromosomal defect. Since there are thousands of genes on each chromosome, this will usually have a disastrous effect leading to embryonic death, often at such an early state that the woman never realizes that she was pregnant. Sometimes the miscarriage occurs after the pregnancy has been confirmed. Several chromosomal studies of such abortuses have revealed that more than half of first trimester abortuses have extra or missing chromosomes.

In rare instances, the chromosomally abnormal fetus survives to birth. The infants, as one might expect from the drastically altered number of genes present, generally have multiple major clinical anomalies as well as mental retardation. The exception is an altered number of X or Y chromosomes, where the clinical manifestations are much less severe.

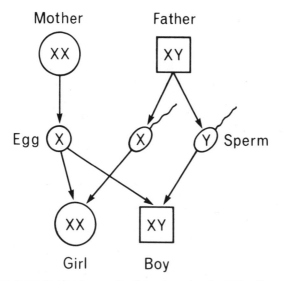

Figure 4. Sex determination in man. An X-bearing sperm fertilizing the ova produces a girl, a Y-bearing sperm produces a boy fetus.

Chromosomal Disorders

Chromosome disorders are called genetic because they involve a defect in the genetic material. Usually, however, they are not inherited from the parents. They are due to new mutations in the eggs or sperms of chromosomally normal parents.

Trisomy 21 or Down's syndrome (Figure 5) is probably the most common major chromosome abnormality. Such an individual has 47 chromosomes, including an extra small autosome, number 21. The syndrome includes mental retardation and several characteristic clinical features: slanted eyes, protruding tongue, and abnormal fingerprint patterns. Heart disease is often part of the syndrome. The risk of having a child with Down's syndrome increases greatly with increased maternal age. This is shown in Figure 6. The risk at 20 years of age is 0.3/1,000, while the risk at 40 is 14/1,000. The risk of other chromosome abnormalities is also somewhat increased with increased maternal age. The overall risk of a child being born with an extra or a missing chromosome is about 1/200.

In 95% of Down's syndrome cases both parents have perfectly normal chromosome complements. As mentioned, increased age predisposes for nondisjunction at the time of the formation of the egg. Other factors, such as maternal hyperthyroidism or exposure to radiation, have also been

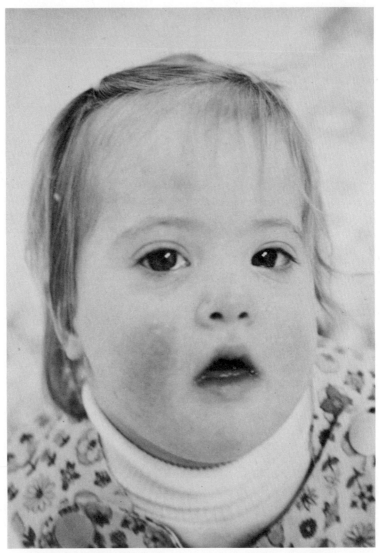

Figure 5. Child with trisomy of chromosome 21, Down's syndrome.

implicated. In a very few cases the defect is truly inherited from one of the parents. In those cases, there has been a rearrangement in the chromosomes called a translocation. This means that a piece of chromosome, in this case number 21, has fused with a portion of another chromosome. This translocation increases the risk of a nondisjunction at the time of the

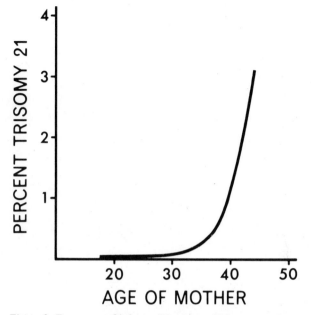

Figure 6. Frequency of infants with trisomy 21 by maternal age.

formation of the eggs or sperms. If such a translocation is present in one of the parents, there are risks for nondisjunction to occur at the time of formation of every germ cell. Although the recurrence risk for normal parents with a Down's syndrome child is only 1 to 2%, the risk for a parent with such a translocation is probably several times higher, perhaps as high as 10%. Therefore, in the family with a child with Down's syndrome it is important to advise a chromosome analysis not only of the child but also of the parents.

There is no cure for Down's syndrome. Even though the intellectual capacity varies in different children, the child will need ongoing supervision throughout his life. Therefore, efforts are made in many medical centers to prevent the birth of such children. Since diagnosis of the chromosome constitution can be done in the 12th to 16th week of pregnancy, all women at risk should be offered this procedure. It is called amniocentesis and involves removal of about 10 cc of the amniotic fluid which contains some fetal cells. These cells can be analyzed both with regard to chromosome content as well as a number of metabolic disorders. The procedure is shown in Figure 7. Since older women have a higher risk than the general population, amniocentesis is offered to pregnant women over 35 years of age in many medical centers. Another high risk group is

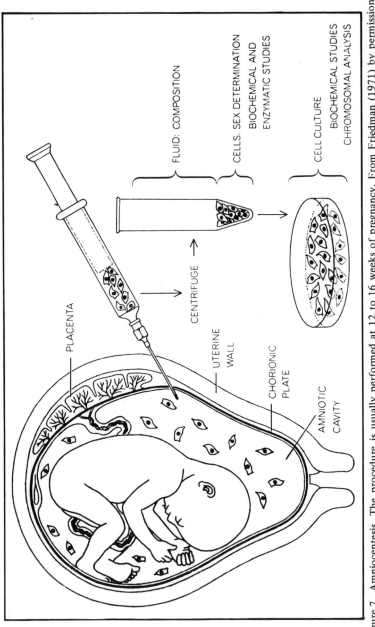

Figure 7. Amniocentesis. The procedure is usually performed at 12 to 16 weeks of pregnancy. From Friedman (1971) by permission of W. H. Freeman & Co., Publishers.

comprised of couples in which one individual is a translocation carrier. A third group which often elects to have amniocentesis consists of women who have already had a child with Down's syndrome. Aside from their recurrence risk of 1 to 2%, their concern is great, having previously experienced the trauma of having an abnormal child. Rather than worry for 9 months, many elect to have the chromosomes of their unborn child analyzed.

Other chromosome abnormalities involving the autosomes include trisomy 8, trisomy 13, trisomy 16, and trisomy 18. All of these disorders include multiple congenital malformations as well as mental retardation. Numerous cases of *partial* trisomies (the normal set of chromosomes plus a part of an extra chromosome) or partial monosomies (a part of one chromosome in the set missing) have also been described. The clinical effects are usually extensive and genetic counseling including information about prenatal diagnosis of chromosomes of future children is advised, even if the recurrence risk, as in Down's syndrome, is low, probably less than 1%. The X and Y chromosome abnormalities have less severe consequences clinically and are, therefore, more compatible with life. The incidence of newborns with nondisjunction of an X or a Y chromosome is about 1/400 births. Many different sex chromosome constitutions have been described, the most common being: 47,XXY (male); 47,XXX (female), and 45,X (female). The number indicates the number of chromosomes in each cell, the normal complement being 45,XX and 46,XY. Usually, the fertility of such individuals is impaired and sometimes, but not always, they are mildly retarded. The most characteristic clinical features found in the 47,XXY male are small testicles, eunochoid proportions, and sometimes gynecomastia (breast development). The 47,XYY males are usually clinically normal although often taller than average males and are, therefore, usually not diagnosed. They have been found more often in penal institutions than in the general population and it is felt that at least some 47,XYY males have tendencies towards violent and criminal behavior. The 47,XXX women also have normal clinical features. The incidence of mental retardation seems to be higher in this group than in the other three groups mentioned. The 45,X female, finally, always has short stature (never taller than 5 feet), primary amneorrhea, poor breast development, and sometimes a webbed neck, low hairline in the back, and other minor features. Approximately one-third of the cases have heart defects. The 47,XXY male and the 45,X female are infertile and are often diagnosed for the first time when they are seen for infertility workup.

As with Down's syndrome, most parents of a child with an extra or a missing X or Y are usually chromosomally normal. The recurrence risk is not known, but probably similar to or only slightly higher than the risk for the general population, which is about 1/400. Although the IQ level of individuals with sex chromosome abnormalities is usually somewhat lower than that of their normal siblings, significant mental retardation is rare. Since there usually are no major abnormalities present, genetic counseling centers around reassuring the parents both with regard to the clinical prognosis of the affected child and explanation of the low recurrence risk. In the 47,XXY male and the 45,X female the infertility problem is usually the most serious problem the family must face. Secondary sex characteristics, such as breast development and even some menstrual bleeding in the 45,X female, can be achieved if hormone treatments are started in the teens.

Prevention of Chromosomal Disorders

If a family has had a child with multiple defects found to be due to a chromosomal abnormality, the question of recurrence risk is often raised. It is then essential to study the chromosomes of the two parents to establish whether one of them is a translocation carrier. If this is the case, the recurrence risk is uncertain, but probably 5 to 30%. This is usually considered to be a high risk, and amniocentesis and abortion of affected fetuses should be discussed. If abortion is unacceptable for the family and the husband is the translocation carrier, the possibility of artificial insemination with an unknown donor should be mentioned. The use of this method is increasing, particularly since there are fewer and fewer babies available for adoption each year. If the parents are chromosomally normal, the chromosomal constitution in their abnormal child was due to a mutation. Mutations, both on the chromosomal and the gene level, are rare and the recurrence risk is probably less than 1% except for Down's syndrome. Even this low risk is considered too high by some couples, particularly in view of the serious consequences. Amniocentesis and abortion of abnormal fetuses are then the only certain means of preventing the birth of a second abnormal child. During the genetic counseling, adoption should also be discussed as an alternative.

DISORDERS DETERMINED BY A SINGLE DEFECTIVE GENE

The two homologues in a chromosome pair contain similar genetic material. A gene determining eye color on one homologue is matched by one determining eye color located on exactly the same place on the other homologue. Therefore, genes for all of the different functions are paired, one gene being of maternal origin and the other of paternal origin. They are not necessarily identical, however. It is possible to inherit a gene for straight hair from the father and a gene for curly hair from the mother, for instance. Such genes that are located at the same place on a chromosome code for the same function are called alleles. There is some controversy about how many gene locations or gene loci there are in man. The estimates vary from 10,000 to 1 million loci. A number of disorders that are attributable to a defect in one single gene locus exceeds 1,000.

Sometimes the characteristic of one allele will dominate in its expression over the allele on the homologue. It is then called a dominant gene. Curly hair is dominant over straight hair. If an individual has a gene for curly hair on one chromosome homologue and a gene for straight hair at the same locus on the other homologue, the individual will show the dominant characteristic, i.e., curly hair. In describing the gene complement of this person, one might write: Hh, H for the dominant gene and h for the other gene, which is called the recessive gene. However, if an individual has the genetic constitution hh, i.e., both homologues contain the recessive gene, then the individual will have straight hair. In other words, it takes only one dominant gene on one of the two homologues to show a dominant characteristic or phenotype, but it takes two recessive genes at the same locus to express the recessive characteristic.

Dominantly Inherited Disorders

Dominantly inherited disorders are characterized by the fact that they are inherited from parent to child. This means that one of the parents usually is affected with the same disorder. Since the parent survived to reproduce, it might mean that the disorder is a mild one. Examples of benign dominant traits are polydactyly (extra fingers), white forelock, and ptosis (droopy eyelids). Another possibility is that the disorder is quite variable in its clinical manifestations. A mildly affected parent could give birth to a severely affected offspring. An example of a clinically extremely variable dominantly inherited disorder is neurofilbromatosis, in which the symptoms may include: neurofibromas anywhere in the body including the brain, scoliosis, mental retardation, malignant tumors, and light brown smooth birth marks called *café-au-lait* spots. Sometimes the birth marks are the only sign of the disease. Von Willebrand's disease is another example. It is a defect in one of the substances responsible for clotting of the blood. The amount of clotting factor may vary in this disorder from complete absence to entirely normal amounts. A third group of dominantly inherited disorders is comprised of those which do not manifest themselves until adult life, perhaps even after the childbearing period. Such a disorder is Huntington's chorea, which is a severe nerve degenera-

Dominant Inheritance

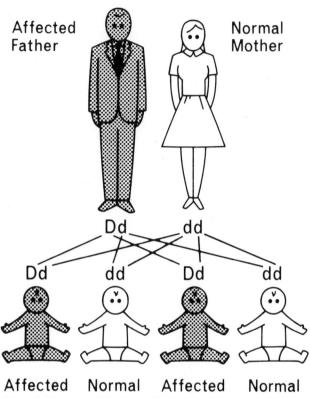

Figure 8. Dominant inheritance. Half of the children are affected.

tive disease starting in the third or fourth decade or even later with tremors, confusion, and altered personality and ending in complete brain degeneration.

The offspring from a mating of an individual with a dominant disorder and a normal individual is shown in Figure 8. On the average, one-half of the children will inherit the abnormal gene and one-half will inherit the normal one. If the affected parent is a woman, she has a 50% chance at each ovulation to release an egg with the mutant gene.

Finally, there are some dominantly inherited disorders that include major congenital malformations and impaired fertility. An example of such a disorder is achondroplasia, which is the most common form of dwarfism, the incidence being about 1/10,000. The clinical features are short arms and legs although the trunk is normal in size and the head is of normal size but with some bossing of the forehead. Intelligence is normal. The fertility is about 30% of normal, partly because of obstetrical complications in affected women and partly because of social reasons. Many affected individuals die in early childhood and, of those who survive to adulthood, many do not marry and have children. Most cases, therefore, are not born to an affected parent but are due to new mutations, both parents being normal. The mutation rate in achondroplasia is one of the highest recorded in man—about 1/20,000 germ cells. The mutation rate seems to be increased with increased paternal age. If this dominant gene is present in both homologues, meaning the gene constitution AA, the condition is lethal. There have been some matings between two achondroplastic dwarfs reported. Of the liveborn offspring, two-thirds will be dwarfs like their parents and one-third will be of normal stature.

Methods of Prevention of Dominantly Inherited Disorders

There are not many dominantly inherited disorders which can be diagnosed *in utero*. Since the majority of disorders are so variable, one would ideally like to know not only whether the fetus is affected or not but also the degree of the phenotypic involvement. If there are bony abnormalities suspected, an oblique x-ray of the pelvis at 20 weeks of gestation might be helpful. Gene linkage will probably be helpful in the future but can at the present time only be used in certain families with myotonic dystrophy, a particular form of muscular dystrophy. The gene for this disorder is located very close to a gene locus called secretor. At this locus, some individuals have a dominant gene which makes their ABO blood group substance secrete into the saliva and it has also been found in the amniotic fluid. If the dystrophic parent has the secretor gene on the same homologue as the gene for the disease but not on the other homologue and the other parent is secretor negative, a test of the amniotic fluid will be valuable. This is demonstrated in Figure 9. If the amniotic fluid test shows the fetus to be secretor positive, the probability is high that it will have inherited not only S but also M and will be affected, since, in this example, S is located on the same homologue and in close proximity to M.

Intensive research is now in progress to find other "linkage groups," i.e., gene loci that are located close together. As the chromosome map gets more complete, the probability of finding genetic markers such as blood groups in close proximity to genes causing disease will increase.

Adoption or, if the gene is inherited in the husband's family, artificial insemination with unknown donor is the most practical solution at the

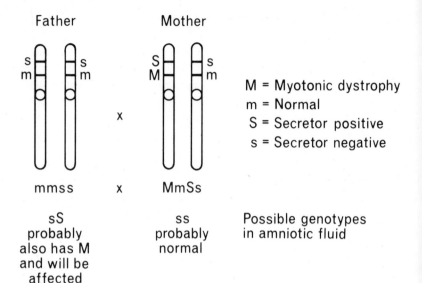

Father   Mother

M = Myotonic dystrophy
m = Normal
S = Secretor positive
s = Secretor negative

mmss   X   MmSs

| sS
probably
also has M
and will be
affected | ss
probably
normal | Possible genotypes
in amniotic fluid |

Figure 9. Detection of a fetus with a high risk of having the gene for myotonic dystrophy.

present time for families who do not want to perpetuate a dominant gene in future generations.

Recessively Inherited Disorders

In recessive disorders, clinically normal parents who carry the gene have clinically affected offspring. The syndromes, therefore, are not directly inherited from parent to child. Two sibs in a family can be affected, however. Males and females are equally often affected.

Recessive disorders are generally much more clinically uniform than the dominant disorders. They are inherited from both parents. The abnormal gene is recessive and the normal gene is dominant. Both parents, although they are carrying the gene, are clinically normal. The different outcomes of the pregnancies are shown in Figure 10. At every pregnancy, there are 3 out of 4 chances to have a clinically normal child and 1 out of 4 that the child will be affected. There is a 2/4 or 50% chance that the child will be normal, but carry the defective gene just like the parents. Of the clinically normal offspring, therefore, 2 out of 3 will be carriers.

The most common, severe recessive disorders are: cystic fibrosis, Tay-Sachs disease, and sickle cell anemia. Cystic fibrosis is the most common in the Caucasian population. The disorder affects lungs and

Recessive Inheritance

Figure 10. Recessive inheritance. Parents are clinically normal. One-quarter of the children are affected.

pancreas with fibrous overgrowth and death occurs before adulthood. The incidence is about 1/20,000 Caucasian births. At the present time, there is no method of identifying the normal carrier of the gene (the carrier frequency is as high as 1/23) and there is no prenatal test to identify the affected fetus.

Tay-Sachs disease is common only in Jewish population of Eastern European origin. The incidence of affected at birth (genotype aa) in the New York Jewish population is about 1/5,000 and the frequency of normal individuals who carry the gene (genotype Aa) is 1/35. The disorder is characterized by developmental retardation, followed by paralysis, dementia, and blindness. Death occurs in the second or third year of life. In this disorder, however, a reliable carrier test has been developed, which can diagnose the affected fetus in the 12th to 16th week of pregnancy. Several communities have organized screening programs in order to identify all couples who are carriers and who, therefore, have a 1 in 4 risk at each pregnancy of having an affected child.

Sickle cell anemia is a disease in which an abnormal hemoglobin is present in the erythrocytes, causing them to sickle. It is most prevalent in the black population. In U.S. blacks the incidence at birth is 1/400 and the carrier frequency is 1/9. A child with this disorder has severe hemolytic anemia and his growth development is retarded. Another characteristic feature is the occurrence of hemolytic crises, in which blood destruction is increased. Abdominal pains and joint pains are common. Death often occurs in childhood; only few affected individuals reach adult life. In sickle cell anemia, a carrier test has been developed which can identify the normal carrier with an Ss genotype. However, there is no prenatal test for the ss homozygote as is the case in Tay-Sachs disease. Genetic counseling to a couple who are both found to be carriers, therefore, concerns itself mostly with the explanation of the clinical prognosis of an affected child and the 1 in 4 risk at each pregnancy. It is important to emphasize that if the first child is affected it does not guarantee that the next 3 children will be normal. Rather there is a 1 in 4 chance at *each* pregnancy.

Phenylketonuria (PKU) is only one of a number of recessively inherited metabolic disorders which have quite a severe effect on the mental development if not diagnosed at birth. Luckily, a very inexpensive test for the disorder has been developed. In most states, therefore, laws have been passed to the effect that every newborn infant is tested for PKU. If an affected child is identified, it will be put on a special low phenylalanine diet (phenylaline is present in protein) for the first several years of life. This treatment will prevent or greatly reduce the degree of mental retardation that would have followed if the child had been on a regular diet. PKU cannot be identified by amniocentesis. This is because the mental retardation is caused by a defect in the breakdown of phenylalanine to tyrosine. Since phenylaline is introduced with food, it is not present until the first feeding after birth. PKU, like most metabolic disorders, is very rare. The incidence is about 1/20,000 births and the carrier frequency is about 1/70. As in most metabolic diseases, there is no reliable method of detecting the carriers at the present time. The normal allele on one of the homologues in the heterozygote carrier (genotype Aa) makes the same amount of product as if both alleles had been normal (AA).

Prevention of Recessively Inherited Disorders

Most recessive disorders are so rare that screening for carriers, even if a carrier test were available, would be both impractical and prohibitively expensive. Most individuals are identified as carriers only when they have their first affected child. The first case in a sibship, therefore, can usually not be prevented. However, in 50 or more rare metabolic disorders there are now methods of prenatal diagnosis available so that a second affected child can be prevented through abortion of an affected fetus. If abortion is unacceptable to the couple, artificial insemination with an unknown donor will lower the risk of a second affected child from 1 in 4 to about 1 in 500 in most cases.

X-linked Recessive Disorders

There are many genes causing abnormalities on the X chromosome. Most of them are recessive. Therefore, females who have two X chromosomes can be carriers of the disorders and not show any clinical symptoms just as in the autosomal recessive disorders described previously. Males, on the other hand, who have only one X, will show the defect if the recessive gene is present on their X chromosome. The Y chromosome has no or very few genes homologous with the X chromosome. There will be no normal gene product produced, since there is no homologous normal gene present. The characteristics of X-linked disorders, therefore, are: only males affected, inheritance through healthy females (no male to male transmission).

A normal male and a carrier female can produce the offspring of four different genotypes as shown in Figure 11A.

There is a 1 in 4 risk at every pregnancy to have an affected son, 1 in 4 to have a carrier daughter who is clinically normal like her mother, and 2 in 4 or 50% to have a genetically normal son or daughter. It should be emphasized that only the mother in this mating is responsible for the risk while the father is completely normal. If an affected male mates with a normal female, the possibilities are as shown in Figure 11B. All daughters will be carriers (and have a 1 in 4 risk in each of their pregnancies) and all sons will be completely normal, since they inherited the normal Y chromosome and not the abnormal X chromosome from their father.

The most common severe disorders with X-linked recessive inheritance are hemophilia A and Duchenne muscular dystrophy. In hemophilia A, the treatments available at the present time have made it possible for affected

X-Linked Inheritance
(Through Carrier Woman)

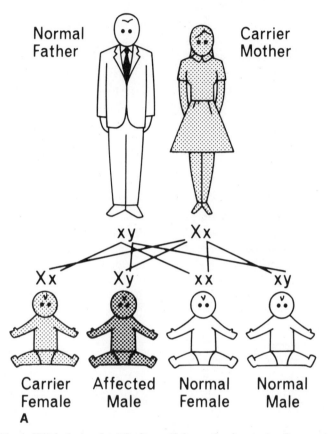

Figure 11. *A*, X-linked recessive inheritance if the mother is a carrier. One-quarter of the children (always boys) are affected. *B*, X-linked recessive inheritance if the father

males to live more normal lives. The treatments include blood concentrates containing the essential clotting factor, which can be kept frozen and administered at the time of bleeding by the patient himself. Most hemophiliacs have no or very little clotting ability in their own blood. The incidence of such severe hemophiliacs at birth is 1/10,000 male births and the carrier frequency is 1/5,000 females. The estimated cost of blood

X-Linked Inheritance
(From Affected Male)

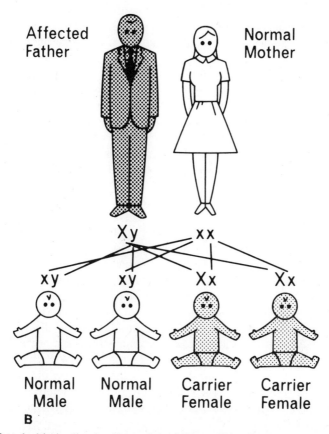

Affected Father

Normal Mother

Xy — XX

xy   xy   Xx   Xx

Normal Male   Normal Male   Carrier Female   Carrier Female

B

is affected with the disorder. None of the children will be affected, but all daughters will be carriers.

product alone for a severe hemophiliac is about $5,000 per year and a simple operation, such as a tooth extraction, costs $1,500 or more since it usually requires a week of hospitalization and repeated transfusions. Therefore, many families that have a child with the disease are most anxious not to have another child affected, even if the probability of an affected boy reaching adulthood now is increased. Although the carrier status of the females can be established with reasonable certainty by a blood test, there is no prenatal test to diagnose an affected male fetus. Work is being done to develop a safe technique of drawing a fetal blood sample through the cord. However, even if this can be accomplished, there is doubt that the clotting factor is being produced in sufficient amounts early in pregnancy. However, sex can be reliably determined early in pregnancy by looking at the fetal chromosomes. Therefore, at the present time some couples elect to abort all male fetuses, since only males are affected.

Duchenne muscular dystrophy is a progressive muscle degeneration starting shortly after birth. It affects 1 in 5,000 males. About half of the affected boys do not start walking until 18 months or later and they often never proceed past the wobbling gait of a child who just learned how to walk. Occasionally, the first 3 years of life are reported to be normal developmentally. Walking becomes more difficult as time goes by. Crutches become necessary and by 10 years of age the boy might be bound to a wheelchair. Mental retardation is sometimes part of the syndrome as is heart disease, since the heart muscle might be involved in the muscle degeneration. Death usually occurs around age 17. There is no known cure for Duchenne muscular dystrophy. A carrier test has been developed but is less accurate at the present time than the one for hemophilia A. Many cases are termed sporadic, because the family history is negative. This is due to the fact that the mutation rate is comparatively high: one-third of all cases are due to a new mutation in the boy fetus and another one-third are due to a new mutation in the mother. In the first case, the recurrence risk is virtually zero, but in the case where the mother is a new mutation the recurrence risk for her future pregnancies will be 1 in 4. Both cases will be labeled "sporadic." Therefore, an accurate carrier test performed on the mother is of great value. If she is not found to be a carrier, the son was a new mutation and the recurrence risk is negligible. If she is found to be a carrier, the risk is 1 in 4.

Prevention of X-linked Recessive Disorders

Only very few X-linked disorders can be diagnosed *in utero*. The most important disorder which can be detected prenatally is Hunter's syndrome or mucopolysaccharidosis type II, which is a severe metabolic disorder. Affected males have coarse features and progressive mental dementia. This disorder can be diagnosed in the amniotic fluid and prevention of affected sibs of an affected male is possible through abortion. Other X-linked disorders can only be prevented by selective abortion of all male fetuses of carrier females. In the near future, it will probably be possible to separate the X- and the Y-bearing sperm through mechanical or chemical means. The carrier will be able to elect artificial insemination with her husband's X-bearing sperm and thus have only daughters. This would obviate the need to abort any male fetuses.

GENETIC ASPECTS OF
SOME COMMON CONGENITAL MALFORMATIONS

About 1 infant of 30 has a serious congenital malformation. Although many chromosomal as well as single gene disorders include congenital malformations, the most common major malformations are not inherited in a simple fashion. They are instead caused by several genes and are also influenced by environmental factors. These environmental factors can be placental conditions, implantation site in the uterus, maternal nutritional factors, maternal drug use, viruses, and many other, often unidentified factors. The etiology of these abnormalities is, therefore, called multifactorial or polygenic. Familial cases have been described, but the recurrence risk is much lower than in single gene disorders. Congenital heart disease, which is present in about 1% of newborn infants, is due to multiple genes about 98% of the time. If a child is born with ventricular septal defect, which is the most common of the malformations, the recurrence risk for other sibs is about 5%. However, if other individuals in the family are affected as well, this recurrence risk increases. If one of the parents is affected, the recurrence risk increases more than if the second individual affected is a more distant relative, such as a first cousin. Therefore, it is very important to obtain a thorough family history and a firm diagnosis on all presumed affected before meaningful genetic counseling can be given. The recurrence risk is also dependent on how common the disorder is in the population. As a rule of thumb, the recurrence risk of a polygenic trait for a subsequent sib is $\sqrt{p}$, where p is the incidence at birth in the population. This is true only if the family history is negative. In other words, if the incidence is $1/1,000$, as is the case with cleft lip with or without cleft palate, the risk of having a second child with the disorder is $\sqrt{1/1,000} = 1/32$ if no other relative is known to have the abnormality. If the woman has a brother with cleft lip but she herself is normal, the risk for her of having an affected child is only slightly increased, probably to about $1/150$.

Another characteristic of polygenic disorders is the fact that the recurrence risk increases with increased severity of the disorder in the proband. If a child has bilateral cleft lip the recurrence risk is greater than that for unilateral cleft lip.

Congenital heart disease and cleft lip and palate have been mentioned as two groups of disorders which are polygenically inherited in the majority of cases. Other malformations include central nervous system defects (spina bifida, hydrocephaly, anencephaly), congenital dislocation of the hip, pyloric stenosis, and nonspecific mental retardation. Adult diseases, such as cardiovascular disorders, hypertensions, and susceptibility to some forms of cancers, are also inherited as multifactorial traits. It should be mentioned, finally, that many normal traits are inherited in this fashion. These include height, hair color, eye color, skin color, and intelligence.

THE ROLE OF PARAMEDICAL PERSONNEL IN GENETICS

There are many functions in a clinical setting that can be satisfactorily carried out by paramedical personnel. In every case of a genetically determined disorder, the family should be given the facts about prognosis and recurrence risk for the couple with the affected child. The risk to the future offspring of the affected child and any of his normal siblings should also be discussed. Consider, as an example, two normal parents who have a child with cleft lip as well as a number of normal children. Upon questioning, they assure you that they have completed their family. This might be correct, but it is still very important to give the couple counseling with regard to the risk of having affected grandchildren and the importance for their children to receive professional genetic counseling before they have a family. Usually, relatives tend to overestimate their risk. An estimate of 50 to 100% is often given when the true figure is 3 to 5%. Needless to say that it will relieve the parents to get the true risk instead of waiting and worrying unnecessarily for years when their child is growing up. Most parents will not come and ask about the risk for their children, however. The physician caring for the child will often not think of bringing up this aspect, since he or she is mostly concerned with the clinical course of the affected child. Therefore, in recent years, the recognition of the importance of a family-oriented person trained in genetics has been made by many medical centers. This is an individual who can recognize the genetic nature of the disorder and reinforce the facts about prognosis and recurrence once the diagnosis is made by the physician.

Although the *primary* counseling session or sessions can be made by a paramedical person if he or she is extremely familiar with the disorder, it is usually given by a person with an M.D. degree. However, it is generally agreed among medical geneticists that one counseling session is insufficient. The psychological trauma is great for the family, and depression and rejection or anger are common reactions. Therefore, the counseling of any family should be a long term project, perhaps over a 6-month or a 1-year period. In the *follow-up period*, paramedical personnel are of great value. They have the time to develop a rapport with the family which is so necessary in psychologically traumatic experiences. Sometimes genetic counseling should be given to families with totally nongenetic problems, i.e., if the family erroneously believes the condition to be inherited and is worried about recurrence.

Before the genetic counseling sessions can be carried out a thorough investigation of the case must take place. This includes a thorough family history with documentation from medical records, etc., of every diagnosis obtained from the informant. It often includes correspondence with other medical centers and consultations with specialists such as radiologists. Paramedical personnel with genetic training are moving into performance of all of these tasks.

Finally, paramedical personnel can make an important contribution with regard to referral of cases for genetic workup in specialty clinics. In this aspect, nurses in particular have an important function. By actively taking an interest in a family, one almost always finds that it is possible to relieve rather than increase the anxiety.

LITERATURE CITED

Friedman, T. 1971. Prenatal diagnosis of genetic disease. Sci. Amer. 225: 34–42.

SUGGESTED READINGS

McKusick, V. A. 1969. Human Genetics. Prentice Hall, International Inc., London.

McKusick, V. A., and R. Claiborne (eds.). 1973. Medical Genetics. HP Publishing Co., Inc., New York.

Nora, J. J., and F. C. Fraser. 1974. Medical Genetics: Principles and Practice. Lea & Feibiger, Philadelphia.

Reed, S. C. Counseling in Medical Genetics. W.B. Saunders Co., Philadelphia.

IV THE HIGH RISK INFANT

Annette Lansford, M.D. *

A child is considered to be at high risk because of adverse genetic, prenatal, perinatal, neonatal, postnatal, or environmental influences which may lead to subsequent development of a handicap or developmental deviation. It is important to note that a handicap is often associated with preceding high risk factors; however, the reverse does not always hold—that is, high risk factors are not necessarily followed by the development of a handicap.

The theoretical merit of the high risk concept is based on the premise that by looking carefully at a group of infants early in life who may have a greater risk of developmental or physical problems, early identification of those with problems, followed by early intervention, leads to a better chance of minimizing the deviation and promoting the child's normal development and maturing process. Therefore, when an infant has been identified as high risk, a careful developmental history, physical and neurological examination, and developmental screening should be done at regular intervals.

In our high risk infant clinic, we have used the high risk concept in a relatively loose and broad sense, with the feeling that a system conducive to over-referral is more acceptable than one leading to an under-referral rate. Below is a list of influences considered to be high risk factors.

FAMILY HISTORY

1. Deafness of genetic origin in parents or siblings.
2. Maternal age over 40—Maternal age has its most striking effect in Down's syndrome, which is much more common in the offspring of mothers over 35. Hydrocephaly is also more frequent in babies born to mothers over 35 years of age. There is also a higher incidence of premature birth in mothers who are 40 years old and older.

---

*Formerly Director of the High Risk Infant Clinic, Pediatric Outpatient Department, University of Colorado Medical Center, Denver, Colorado. Currently practicing developmental pediatrics, Carle Clinic, 602 West University, Urbana, Illinois 61801.

3. Maternal age under 16—In one study it was found that in women 15 years of age and younger, one-fourth were delivered before 36 weeks. Very young mothers also show a higher risk of having toxemia of pregnancy.

Furthermore, malformations affecting the central nervous system are more frequent in the babies born to women who are at the beginning or at the end of reproductive life.

4. History of previous stillbirths—The combined stillbirths and infantile death rate for the siblings of children suffering from diplegic cerebral palsy is approximately twice that expected in the community.

5. History of previous children with congenital malformations—A mother who has had one child with congenital malformations runs a considerably increased risk of producing another child with congenital malformations, although not necessarily of the same type. After having one child with spina bifida, a mother has 12 times the standard risk. After having one child with anencephaly, she has 6 times the standard risk in a subsequent pregnancy. Anencephaly is a developmental anomaly characterized by complete absence of the brain or the presence of small masses attached to the base of the skull.

6. Low socioeconomic class—The percentage of premature births is highest in women of the lower socioeconomic groups.

7. History of a hereditary, metabolic, muscle, or neurological disease in the family such as phenylketonuria, Duchenne's muscular dystrophy, Tay-Sachs disease, etc.

PRENATAL

1. History of maternal rubella or other viral infection in the first 4 months of pregnancy.

2. Toxoplasmosis—This is a parasitic infection, probably a protozoa.

3. Threatened abortion or antepartum hemorrhage—Antepartum hemorrhage or third trimester hemorrhage is an important factor in the prematurity and neonatal death rates. The presence of hemorrhage in the last trimester should always be regarded seriously.

PERINATAL

1. Short gestation (prematurity)—Live born infants delivered before 37 weeks from the first day of the last menstrual period are considered to have a shortened gestational period.

2. Low birth weight (below the 10th percentile for gestational age)— Infants who weigh 2,500 grams (5 pounds, 8 ounces) or less at birth are

considered to have had either a short gestational period, a less than expected rate of intrauterine growth, or both, and are termed as infants of low birth weight.

Prematurity and low birth weight are usually seen together, particularly in infants weighing 1,500 grams (2 pounds, 11 ounces) or less at birth, and are associated with a greater death rate and a greater rate of neonatal problems. Though the statistics vary according to which population is surveyed, generally the incidence of low birth weight infants runs from 6 to 16 percent, about half of which are babies who are not premature or are "small for dates" babies.

Retrolental fibroplasia is a type of toxicity to the retina of the eye caused by an excessive exposure of the retina vessels to oxygen. This is primarily a problem of low birth weight babies because of their greater incidence of pulmonary problems and subsequent requirement for oxygen. If the oxygen has been at a high level for long periods of time and becomes toxic to the eye vessels, blindness can result. There are several stages in the development of retrolental fibroplasia, including intense retinal vasoconstriction, peripheral vasoproliferation, edema of the retina, and vasodilatation and fibrosis.

Chronic oxygen toxicity to the lungs also occurs, most often in low birth weight infants who have required long term oxygen therapy. Bronchopulmonary dysplasia is an entity in which a tremendous proliferation of cells occurs which bulge out into the respiratory bronchioles because of epithelial injury. These infants are often oxygen dependent at the time of discharge from the nursery and require oxygen for long periods of time before they can gradually be weaned from it.

Low birth weight babies frequently never catch up in height and weight with their normal peers. Most low birth weight babies are significantly smaller than their normal birth weight peers at the end of the first year of life.

The death rate of low birth weight infants who survive to be discharged from the hospital nursery is 3 times that of full term infants during the first 2 years of life. Many of these deaths are caused by infections. There is a high incidence of handicaps, both neurological and mental (among small prematures).

3. Moderate to severe asphyxia—Asphyxia, anoxia, and hypoxia are all terms loosely applied to indicate the end result of lack of oxygen from a number of causes. It is the leading cause of perinatal death or permanent damage to the central nervous system. One cause of fetal hypoxia or asphyxia is the compression of the umbilical cord between the presenting part and the pelvic tissues during the process of labor and delivery. Other

causes of fetal anoxia are inadequate oxygenization of maternal blood, low maternal blood pressure, inadequate relaxation of the uterus to permit placental filling, and inadequate attachment of the placenta and placental inadequacy as in toxemia and postmaturity.

4. Presence of congenital abnormality—It is a general principle that any major congenital anomaly carries with it a risk of mental subnormality. Major congenital anomalies include defects of skeleton and skull, congenital defects of eyes and ears, congenital heart disease, various congenital skin defects, diseases involving muscle, endocrine defects (such as cretinism), other metabolic conditions (such as amino acid diseases), and mixed genetic and chromosomal defects.

5. Polyhydramnios—The presence of polyhydramnios is often associated with prematurity and/or fetal anomaly such as anencephaly, spina bifida, hydrocephaly, or gastrointestinal tract anomalies.

6. Evidence of fetal distress—A diagnosis of fetal distress is made if the fetal heart tones are in excess of 170 beats per minute or under 110 beats per minute. The normal fetal heart rate is 120 to 160 beats per minute. Another indication of fetal distress is when meconium staining occurs. Meconium is the sticky substance present in the gastrointestinal tract of the fetus. The presence of hypoxia probably leads to the relaxation of the anal sphincter, allowing meconium to pass into the amniotic fluid.

NEONATAL

1. Serum bilirubin over 20 mg/100 ml or an exchange transfusion—Bilirubin is a product of red blood cell breakdown and can be toxic to the newborn brain if it reaches high levels. There are several causes of high bilirubin, the most severe being Rh incompatibility. The contact of the mother's red blood cells with the baby's (which happens when mother's blood crosses the placenta during the birth process) causes the baby's red cells to break down, producing high bilirubin levels. If the bilirubin reaches a high enough level (usually around 20 mg/100 ml in a full term infant) an exchange transfusion is done, which replaces about 50 percent of the baby's blood with blood typed to match the mother. This temporarily delays further red blood cell breakdown in the baby. Any child whose bilirubin level has risen high enough to have necessitated an exchange transfusion is at risk of having brain damage due to bilirubin toxicity. The most severe type of bilirubin central nervous system toxicity is called kernicterus. These babies are usually severely retarded, have cerebral palsy, and have a hearing deficit.

2. An unsatisfactory postnatal state in the infant, particularly when accompanied by any of the following factors—

a. Toxemia—Toxemia of pregnancy is a disorder in which the mothers present with one or more of the following signs: high blood pressure, edema, or protein in the urine. The most severe form of toxemia is eclampsia, in which convulsions and/or coma occur in the mother. Babies of toxemic mothers are at much higher risk.

b. Postmature birth—Postmature births are those in which the babies are born after a gestation of more than 42 weeks. These babies are often small for gestational age and have a higher incidence of neonatal problems. When postmaturity exceeds 3 or more weeks, there is a significant increase in mortality.

c. Abnormal presentation—The normal presentation for a baby during the birth process is the head down with the occiput anterior. Abnormal presentations which often cause difficult deliveries are breech (in which one or both feet are first, or the rear is first), transverse lie (cross-ways), or chin, shoulder, or forehead first.

d. Forceps deliveries—Forceps deliveries can be the cause of a facial palsy (usually only temporary) in the newborn baby. More importantly, forceps are most commonly used in difficult deliveries, which is a high risk factor in itself.

e. Cesarean section—Almost all indications for cesarean section as the method of delivery are high risk events themselves. Indications for a cesarean section include: any cause of delay in labor, fetal distress, severe toxemia, severe high blood pressure during pregnancy, diabetes in the mother, history of repeated stillbirths after vaginal delivery with no specific cause being found, Rh incompatibility, carcinoma of the cervix in the mother, and previous cesarean sections.

f. Maternal diabetes—A high frequency of intrauterine fetal death often prompts the preterm delivery of infants of diabetic mothers by cesarean section. These babies are more prone to the development of low blood sugar (because the mother's high blood glucose levels have stimulated the baby's pancreas to produce high insulin levels) and hyaline membrane disease. There also seems to be an increased frequency of congenital malformations in the fetuses of pregnant diabetics.

3. Difficulty in sucking or swallowing—The failure to feed well may be the first sign of an infection in the newborn. It also may be an early sign of cerebral palsy or mental deficiency.

4. Failure to thrive, not explained by simple feeding problems—It is well

known that mentally defective children tend to be small in stature. Children with congenital infections or chromosomal abnormalities, particularly, fail to thrive.

5. Convulsions—These point to a disorder of the central nervous system.

6. Cyanotic attacks or severe apneic spells—Cyanosis usually indicates respiratory insufficiency, which may be due to primary lung disease or intracranial hemorrhage. If it persists several days, it suggests congenital heart disease.

7. Phenylketonuria (PKU)—PKU is an inherited metabolic disease which, if untreated, causes mental retardation, seizures, growth retardation, and eczema. It can be fairly well controlled by dietary treatment, that is, by giving very little of the amino acid, phenylalanine, which the child cannot metabolize properly. If untreated, the phenylalanine rises to high levels in these children, and is quite toxic to their central nervous system.

8. Abnormal neurological signs in the neonatal period—Examples of this would be poor moro reflex, high pitched cry, spasticity or extreme floppiness, poor suck, etc.

9. Severe illness such as meningitis and encephalitis—Meningitis is an infection of the meninges, which are the enveloping tissues around the brain and spinal cord. Bacterial meningitis not uncommonly leaves residue such as mental retardation, deafness, cranial nerve palsies, etc. Encephalitis is an infection of the brain tissue itself.

POSTNATAL

1. History of physical or emotional abuse of the child.

2. Microcephaly (small head size) noted consistently over a period of time.

3. Macrocephaly (large head size) noted consistently over a period of time.

4. Funny-looking kid (FLK)—Any child with a peculiar appearance should be assessed for neurological and developmental problems.

ENVIRONMENTAL

1. Single parent.

2. Very young mother (under 17 years).

3. Premature child or very sick newborn who had a long hospital stay.

4. Large family.

5. Low socioeconomic class coupled with other high risk factors. It has been shown that low birth weight infants born into middle class socioeco-

nomic groups with well educated parents do well, in marked contrast to the low birth weight infants born into the low socioeconomic class, who do significantly less well in both growth and development.

6. Observed poor mother-child interaction.
7. History of child abuse in a sibling.
8. Historical poor relationship of the mother with her mother.
9. History of psychiatric illness in one or both parents.

FOLLOW-UP OF HIGH RISK INFANTS

Infants who have one or more significant high risk factors in their history should be followed closely in several areas.

1. Growth, height, weight, and head circumference, correcting for prematurity—(Example: if the child was born 4 weeks early or at 36 weeks gestation, subtract 1 month from his chronological age when plotting his growth parameter.)

If the head circumference, height, or weight is rapidly crossing percentile lines on the growth chart, either up or down, the child should be investigated further.

2. Complete physical examination.

3. Frequent developmental screenings—This can be done by using the Denver Developmental Screening Test, the Gesell Infant Scales, the Developmental Screening Inventory, or a similar device. The premature should be corrected for his length of prematurity when assessing his development. It is important to look at the quality of the child's performance on a screening test as well as whether he passes or fails. Not infrequently children may have an abnormal means of accomplishing a task which must be noted (an example is the hypertonic child who bears weight early, for a pathological reason).

4. Careful neurological evaluations—These need not be done by a neurologist, but can be done by any competent health professional who has the knowledge of the normal time sequence of the development and disappearance of the primitive reflexes and the development of automatic responses, in addition to the traditional neurological examination.

Asymmetrical primitive reflexes, persistence of primitive reflexes after their usual disappearance, or delay in the development of automatic responses are often early indicators of a significant motor problem before gross abnormalities in muscle tone or movement are apparent.

It is essential as part of the neurological examination to assess how the child performs in a *functional* way; for example, observe whether the

9-month-old child has a well developed pincer grasp, whether the 12-month-old child drags one foot when walking, etc. These observations will often help identify subtle neurological abnormalities which may be interfering with the child's development and are not apparent on the routine neurological examination.

5. Assessment of the maternal-child interaction—Mothers not infrequently have difficulty in making an attachment to their high risk infant, particularly to those who have been sick and required long stays in the nursery and to those who have developmental delays. These children commonly are viewed as quite fragile and may not be as responsive or gratifying to their mother, making it difficult for her to relate in a warm, loving, and comfortable manner. As these children often have greater needs for stimulation, it is important to assess the maternal-child interaction on each visit. If distance is noted in the relationship, the professional should attempt to help the mother become more comfortable and more involved with her child.

It is suggested that all premature infants have an ophthalmological examination by an ophthalmologist in the first 6 months of age because of the higher risk of visual problems in this group. It is also recommended that every child who has a history of significant hyperbilirubinemia, therapy with antibiotics which are known to be ototoxic, a family history of deafness, a lack of response to the bell, or delayed language development should have a formal audiogram.

One means of following this group of high risk children in a comprehensive manner is through a high risk infant clinic, using a multidisciplinary approach. However, often such a specialty clinic is not available. A pediatrician, an allied health associate, or a nurse can follow the high risk child in a comprehensive manner by looking at the above suggested areas. It is recommended that these areas be looked at frequently during the first 18 months of life. This can be done at the time of routine checks and immunizations, such as 1 to 2 weeks after discharge from the nursery, then every 6 to 8 weeks thereafter until 6 months of age, and then again at 9 months, 12 months, and 18 months. If developmental lags or neurological abnormalities are noted, the child should be referred for a more extensive assessment and early intervention.

Some states have a high risk registry, where infants who are considered to be at high risk are registered and then watched more closely. The risk register concept assumes that a small group of infants, suitably selected, will include most children who will subsequently develop handicapping conditions. A risk register includes a proportion, ideally not more than 20 percent of the total population, selection for the register being based on the defined criteria being an increased risk of developing handicaps. Cerebral palsy, visual defects, auditory defects, and mental retardation are the broad groups of handicaps that have been particularly associated with the risk register approach.

It appears very appropriate that nurses, whether institutional or public health, become quite involved with these children and families on a long term basis.

SUGGESTED READINGS

Battaglia, F. C., and L. O. Lubchenco. 1967. A practical classification of newborn infants by weight and gestational age. J. Pediat. 71: 159.

Beintema, D. J. 1968. A neurological study of newborn infants. Clin. Devel. Med. No. 28.

Cooke, R. E., and S. Levine. 1968. The Biologic Basis of Pediatric Practice. McGraw-Hill Book Co., New York.

Dargassies, St. 1966. Neurological maturation of the premature infant of 23 to 41 weeks gestational age. In F. Falkner (ed.), Human Development. W. B. Saunders Co., Philadelphia.

Drillien, C. M. 1964. The Growth and Development of the Prematurely Born Infant. The Williams & Wilkins Co., Baltimore.

Hoskins, T., and J. E. Squires. 1973. Developmental assessment: A test for gross motor and reflex development. Phys. Ther. J.53 (2).

Nelson, W. E., V. E. Vaughn, and J. R. McKay. 1975. Textbook of Pediatrics. W. B. Saunders Co., Philadelphia.

Paine, R., et al. 1964. Evolution of postural reflexes in normal infants and in the presence of chronic brain syndrome. Neurology. 14(11).

Paine, R. S., and T. E. Oppé. 1966. Neurological Examination of Children. Clinics in Developmental Medicine. Heinemann Imported Books, New York.

V
NORMAL MOTOR DEVELOPMENT IN THE INFANT

Linda Lord, R.P.T., M.P.H. *

Normal motor development proceeds in an orderly sequence in a cephalo-caudal progression and from mass, reflexive movements to specific, voluntary movements. This orderly sequence is dependent upon an intact and normally maturing central nervous system.

The newborn evidences innumerable reflexive patterns which later blend into voluntary patterns of movement and become unrecognizable as the reflexes themselves. These reflexes and early reactions are necessary for the beginning of movement, development of muscle tone and the postural system, and for avoiding noxious stimuli.

The normal infant is flexor tone predominate and moves toward developing more and more extensor tone in the first year of life, in his ability to hold his head, extend his trunk and legs, and then walk. Extensor tone develops first in the head and shoulders as evidenced by the infant's ability to prop on his forearms around 2 months of age. Full extension of the trunk and legs does not develop until the infant reaches 5 to 6 months of age, at which time he is capable of the pivot prone position, allowing him to swivel around using his stomach as a pivot point. Primary reflex responses give way to more mature secondary balance and righting reactions as we see the normal infant develop the basic motor patterns such as head and trunk control, sitting balance, coordination of the arms and then hands, ability to locomote by crawling or hitching, pulling to stand, and walking. These basic patterns of movement in different combinations are changed and adapted into more complex motor skills that are later seen in the 3- to 4-year-old.

There is an increasing need for physicians, nurses, and therapists to know the developmental motor milestones and the reflexes and patterns of movement on which they are based in order to recognize as early as

---

*Chief Physical Therapist, John F. Kennedy Child Development Center; Instructor, Department of Physical Medicine and Rehabilitation, University of Colorado Medical Center, 4200 East 9th Avenue, Denver, Colorado 80220.

possible the deviations from normal. The need for early identification of abnormal movement patterns in order to offer stimulation or therapeutic intervention to infants and interpretation of delayed development to patients has also been stressed for many years. Improved screening abilities are necessary for all medically related professionals because of the increased number of individuals providing well and sick child care.

The major reflexes and reactions noted in the first year of life with their accompanying relationship to normal and abnormal development are presented below and in Tables 1 through 3. Notation that a reflex is or is not present without relating this finding to the developmental status of the infant can only give one a partial picture of the infant. When the examiner understands the relationship between the presence or absence of a reflex and the development or lack of development of motor milestones, his data are more significant and helpful in describing an infant and understanding his individual development and level of functioning.

KEY FOR REFLEX TESTING

Primitive Reflexes–Brainstem

1. Sucking Reflex   Finger placed on lips results in immediate sucking motion of lips; jaw drops and lifts rhythmically.

2. Rooting Reflex   Corner of mouth lightly stroked outwards results in lower lip dropping at that corner. On continuation of this contact to cheek, tongue moves towards stimulus and head turns to follow it.

3. Foot Grasp   Supine–Pressure given to the ball of the foot with examiner's finger results in the toes grasping.

Standing–Stimulation of the sole of the foot by contact with the table results in toes grasping.

4. Hand Grasp   Supine–Placing a finger in the infant's hand from the ulnar side results in fingers closing over the examiner's finger.

5. Asymmetrical Tonic Neck Reflex (ATNR)   Supine–Rotation of the head to the side (90°) results in flexion of the arm on the skull side and extension of arm on face side. Take careful note. If no motion occurs note increase in flexor tone on skull side and increase in extensor tone on face side.

Quadruped–Check for this reflex in the same manner in the quadruped position, when he can maintain the all-four position (at approximately 7 months).

6. Crossed Extension   Supine–Extend one leg with pressure at the thigh. At the same time, stroke the sole of the foot of the extended leg.

Fully present if opposite leg flexes and abducts, then extends and adducts.

Partially present if opposite leg flexes and extends.

7. *Tonic Labyrinthine* Supine—Placement of the body in the supine position results in extension of the upper and lower limbs with minimal flexion of these extremities. When this is strong, the increase in extensor tone is also evidenced by difficulty in placing the arms and legs in flexion.

Prone—Placement of the body in the prone position results in flexion of the upper and lower limbs with minimal extension of these extremities. When this is strong, the increase in flexor tone is also evidenced by difficulty in placing the arms and legs in extension.

8. *Symmetrical Tonic Neck Reflex (STNR)* Place patient in the quadruped position. Passive *extension* of the head results in increased extension of the arms and flexion of the hips. Passive *ventroflexion* of the head results in increased flexion of the arms and extension of the hips.

9. *Stepping Reflex* Holding the infant under his arms in the standing position and leaning him forward result in automatic walking steps that are rhythmical and demonstrate a heel strike.

10. *Placing Reaction* Holding the infant under his arms in the standing position so that the dorsum of the foot brushes the edge of the table results in the foot being lifted and placed upon the table top.

11. *Positive Supporting Reaction* Holding the infant under his arms to bounce him on his feet elicits *extension* of both lower limbs with plantar flexion of feet.

This reaction may also elicit *extension* of both lower limbs followed by *flexion* of the hips and knees.

12. *Moro Reflex* Holding the patient in a semi-sitting position by supporting his back and head and allowing the head to fall backwards (20° to 30°) by releasing support of the head result in complete Moro. This is a sudden extension and abduction of upper extremities, with opening of the hands, followed by flexion to the midline.

Midbrain Righting Reactions

13. *Head Righting Reaction* Holding patient upright under his arms and tilting him 45° laterally result in bringing his head back to the midline. Test to both sides.

14. *Body Righting on Body Reaction* Supine—Passively rotate the shoulder or hip. This results in *segmental* rotation of shoulders, trunk, and pelvis.

15. *Landau Reaction* Prone—Suspend patient by holding him under upper thorax. This results in: a) first stage Landau, extension of head

Table 1. Major reflexes and their relationship to normal and abnormal fine motor and gross motor development

Primary reflexes	Normal	Abnormal
Hand grasp–tactile – Stimulation of the palm elicits reflexive closure over the object.	Part of the total flexion pattern noted in the first 3 months of life. Should disappear with the development of increased extensor tone.	Retention of reflex prevents voluntary grasp and release of objects and development of mature grasping patterns (pincer grasp) (10–12 mo.).
Moro reflex–head Head and shoulders are raised from table and head is dropped back suddenly. Arms, fingers abducted, extended and externally rotated, followed by return to flexion.	This reflex persists approximately 0–4 months. Should disappear with better head control and protective reactions forward in sitting.	Persistence past 4 months of age may prevent the infant from developing good sitting balance, forward protective reactions in sitting and the parachute.
Postural reflexes 1. *Asymmetrical tonic neck reflex (ATNR)* Turning of the head by examiner evokes extension of arm on the face side, flexion of the arm on the skull side (fencer's posture). Legs often affected in the same manner as the arms.	Noted in the first 4 months of life, but *never* an obligatory response in a normal infant nor does it interfere with activities such as turning, or getting hands to mouth. Serves to create an awareness of two sides of body and beginning of eye-hand coordination.	Too strong a reaction or retention of reflex prevents getting hands to midline (3 mo.), rolling back to side (3–4 mo.), hand-to-mouth activities and symmetrical movements of the limbs if head is turned.

2. *Tonic labyrinthine reflex* A. Prone or face-lying position in and of itself produces flexor tone in all extremities.	Normal flexor tone noted in newborn (fetal position). Begins to disappear with development of extensor tone (2–5 months).	Retention of reflex prevents extension in prone for head control and on elbows position (2 mo.), pivot prone and Landau reaction requiring full extension (5–6 mo.).
B. Supine or back-lying position in and of itself produces extensor tone in all extremities.	Development of extensor tone for kicking in supine and total extension (opposite of fetal positioning).	Retention of reflex may cause opisthotonic posturing (total extension with arching of the back) in severe cases. May prevent getting hands to midline and mouth because of retraction of the scapulae (2–3 mo.), rolling supine to prone (3–5 mo.), raising head in anticipation to being picked up (5 mo.), playing with feet when backlying (5 mo.).
3. *Positive supporting reflex* Child held vertically under arms and bounced on balls of feet.	In first 2–4 mo. reflex extension of legs and some weight bearing are noted. Between 5–7 months, extension of legs is followed by flexors and kicking responses. This becomes a more voluntary standing response from 6 months on.	Rigid extension with plantar flexion is almost never seen in a normal infant after the first 4 months of life. Rigid extension with scissoring is usually an abnormal response at any age. Retention of this reflex will prevent normal reciprocal movements of the legs necessary in walking. Retention of this reflex may cause toe walking when the child begins to walk and interfere with balance reactions in standing.

Table 2. Major reflexes and their relationship to normal and abnormal fine motor and gross motor development

Secondary reflexes	Normal	Abnormal
1. Automatic head righting a. When held supported under stomach, head extends at least in line with rest of body. b. When held in sitting, infant holds head steadily. c. When held in vertical position under arms and tilted sideways, head returns to midline to correct for body position.	a. Newborn to 2 mo. Head in line with body or above. Important beginning stages of head control. This is an *automatic*, not a learned response. b. Between 2–4 months, infant shows increased ability to hold head steadily. This is an *automatic*, not a learned response. c. Between 4–6 months, infant shows increased ability to bring head to midline. Responses become increasingly faster with the older infant. This is an *automatic*, not a learned response.	a. Cannot raise head in line with body but flexes over examiner's hand. Demonstrates poor optical and labyrinthine righting and is delayed in head control. b. Inability to keep head in midline even momentarily. Head falls to side, forward or backward with no correction by infant. Indicates delay in head control and presence of weakness in muscles or retention of primary reflexes. c. Child will show poor head and trunk control, and difficulty with sitting balance without his automatic head righting response.
2. Landau reaction Suspend the child by holding him face down under his upper thorax.	1st stage—1–3 mo. Extension of head above shoulder level. 2nd stage—3–6 mo. Extension of head and thorax. 3rd stage—6–12 mo. Extension of head, trunk, hips, and legs. Full extension at this age (6–12 months) indicates the ability to maintain the upright posture.	Rigid extension of head, trunk and legs in the first 2 months may be early signs of hypertonicity. Flexion of the trunk over the examiner's hand instead of extension indicates abnormal hypotonia. The inability to extend the head and trunk at 6 months will delay sitting and walking.

3. Protective reactions

Protective reactions appear in response to a sudden displacing force and are in the same direction as the force.

These are normal responses, not learned skills.

a. Sitting

1) Forward—child's balance in sitting is suddenly disturbed forwards by pushing the child from the back.

1) Forward—arms will immediately move forward and the child will prop on arms (4–6 mo.). This response will improve with age.

No response in an attempt to protect oneself at expected age will delay sitting and walking and may be indicative of retention of some primary reflexes.

2) Lateral—child's balance in sitting is suddenly disturbed by pushing the child sideways.

2) Lateral—arm on side closest to supporting surface will reach out to catch the child (6–8 mo.). This response should be equal to *both sides and improve with age.*

Unequal protective responses, that is, elicited to one side and not the other may indicate one-sided involvement such as a hemiparesis or a strong asymmetrical tonic neck reflex.

3) Backwards—child's balance in sitting is suddenly disturbed by pushing the child from the front.

3) Backwards—arm will reach backwards to break the anticipated fall, with rotation of the trunk and forward flexion of the legs (8–12 mo.). This response usually is present before walking can be anticipated.

Consistently slow responses in any direction are usually reflected in a child's delayed motor development.

b. Parachute or Protective Extension Forward

Child is held by waist up-ended and moved quickly toward the table or floor.

b. Child's upper limbs and fingers abduct and extend as if to protect his head. Fully developed parachute is anticipated by 9 mo., but a partial reaction can be seen by 4–5 mo.

b. No reaction by 5–6 mo. is of concern. Child may retract his arms in response and this may be indicative of a poorly integrated Moro or other primitive reflex. Some delays in sitting and walking may be noted.

95

Table 3. Reflex developments (/ / = most accepted range; - - - = upper or lower limits)

		NB	1	2	3	4	5	6	7	8	9	10	11	12
Primitive reflexes (brain stem)														
1 Suck		//	//	//	//	//	//	//	---	---	---	---		
2 Root		//	//	//	//	//	//	---	---	---	---	---		
3 Foot grasp	L	//	//	//	//	//	//	//	---	---	---			
	R	//	//	//	//	//	//	//	//	//	//			
4 Hand grasp	L	//	//	//	//	//	---	---	---	---	---	---		
	R	//	//	//	//	//	---	---	---	---	---	---		
5 ATNR														
Supine (posture)	L		//	//	//	//	---	---						
	R		//	//	//	//	---	---						
Supine (tone)	L		//	//	//	//	---	---						
	R		//	//	//	//	---	---						
*Quadruped position	L			//	//	//								
	R			//	//	//								
6 X-Extension	L	//	//	---										
	R	//	//	---										
Partial		//	//	---										
Full	L	//	//											
	R	//	//											
7 Tonic	P	//	//	//	//	//	---	---	---	---	---	---		
Labyrinthine	S	//	//	//	//	//	---	---	---	---	---	---		
8 STNR														
head extension							//	//	//					
head ventroflexion						---	//	//						
9 STEP		//	//			---	//	//	//	//	//	//	//	//
10 PLACE		//	//	//	//	//	//	//	//	//	//	//	//	//

11 Positive support										
Extension	L				//	//	//	--	--	--
Extension	R				//	//	//	--	--	--
flexion	L				//	//	//	//	//	//
	R				//	//	//	//	//	//
12 MORO										
Complete		//	//	//	//	//	//	--	--	
Partial		//	//	//	//	//	//	--	--	
Mid brain righting reactions										
13 Head Vert.	L	--	//	//	//	//	//	//	//	//
	R	--	//	//	//	//	//	//	//	//
14 Body on body rotation	L		//	//	//	//	//	//	//	//
	R		//	//	//	//	//	//	//	//
15 Landau										
Head				//	//	//	//	//	//	//
Head and thorax					//	//	//	//	//	//
Head, thorax, and legs					//	//	//	//	//	
Protective reactions										
16 Downward	L			//	//	//	//	//	//	//
	R			//	//	//	//	//	//	//
17 Sideways arms	L				//	//	//	//	//	//
	R				//	//	//	//	//	//
18 Backward arms	L					//	--	//	//	
	R					//	--	//	//	
19 Parachute	L					//	//	//	//	
	R					//	//	//	//	

*No norms for this. Reference: Milani-Comparetti and Gidoni (1967.)

above shoulder level; b) second stage Landau, extension of head and thorax; c) third stage Landau, extension of head, trunk, hips, and legs.

Protective Reactions

16. Downward Legs Holding the patient under the arms, lift him up and rapidly lower him towards the table. This results in extension, abduction, and external rotation of the legs.

17. Protective Extension–Sideways Place patient in sitting position. Pushing him sideways off balance will result in abduction of the opposite arm with extension of elbow, wrist, and fingers.

18. Protective Extension–Backwards Place patient in sitting position. Pushing him backwards results in: a) Full reaction—Backward extension of both arms; b) Partial reaction—Trunk rotation with backward extension of one arm.

19. Parachute Hold patient at the waist, up end and move him rapidly downward towards the table. This results in immediate extension of arms with abduction and extension of fingers as if protecting the head.

"RED FLAGS": Concerns to Later Development

The following is a listing of "red flags" in the newborn period that should be noted and observed as possible concerns to later development.

1. Asymmetrical findings—Newborn shows symmetrical and equal development.
    a. Fisting on one side—Hemiparesis should be ruled out.
    b. Asymmetrical Moro responses—Hemiparesis should be ruled out.
2. Absence of primary reflexes such as Moro, hand grasp—This may indicate poor cerebral development or cerebral damage.
3. Lack of spontaneous movements—This may indicate paralysis or weakness.
4. Extreme jitteriness—This may be early signs of hypertonicity or a sensitive child. The child will need special handling, with mother given extra support.
5. Extremes of muscle tone—Either hypotonia or hypertonia could indicate cerebral damage.
6. Scissoring of the lower extremities—This may indicate increased tone or a strong positive supporting reflex.
7. Excessive fisting—Too strong a grasp reflex may be interfering with normal opening of the hands at rest and other relaxed times of the day.

SUGGESTED READINGS

Fiorentino, M. R. 1972. The influence of primitive reflexes on motor development. *In* Normal and Abnormal Development. Charles C. Thomas, Publisher, Springfield, Ill.

Milani-Comparetti, A., and E. A. Gidoni. 1967. Routine developmental examination in normal and retarded children. Devel. Med. Child Neurol. 9: 631.

Paine, R. S., T. B. Brazelton, D. Donovan, J. E. Drobaugh, J. Hubbell, and E. M. Lears. 1964. Evolution of postural reflexes in normal infants and in the presence of chronic brain syndromes. Neurology 4: 1035.

VI
VISION
SCREENING

*Cyndi Thero**

As with all forms of health screenings, testing for visual problems should be an organized, worthwhile, pleasant experience for both the individual being screened and the personnel doing the testing. There are a variety of tests that can be administered in a screening program. The techniques used in administering the tests vary a great deal, depending on the age of the individual being screened. Screening procedures can be divided into two approaches: first, testing a preschooler (ages 3 through 6); and second, testing school-age children and adults.

Two types of screening that can be administered include: 1) a single unit screening, or 2) a multiphasic vision screening procedure. An example of a single unit screening would be to test an individual for one particular type of visual problem such as central vision acuity. In using a multiphasic vision screening, testing is done for various visual problems such as central visual acuity, hyperopia (farsightedness), myopia (nearsightedness), color blindness, muscle imbalance, and depth perception. Whichever form of screening is chosen, the tester must fully understand how to administer the various tests and how to handle the results efficiently. Remember, a screening is only as good as the results and how they are followed up. The screening will be of little value if provision is not made for a thorough follow-up on the individuals who failed any portion of the screening administered.

There are several types of tests available for testing central visual acuity. The test should be simple yet accurate in order that a 3-year-old child can be screened proficiently. When testing with a figure chart the child may not be familiar with the vocabulary of the pictures that are being shown. One cannot assume anything in screening.

On setting up an area for screening the most important factor is lighting. If the lighting is not adequate, the purpose in vision screening is defeated. If in a room with windows and sunlight, close the drapes or blinds and use artificial lighting. Sunlight casts too much glare, on or

---

*Consultant/Screening Specialist, Unique Systems Corporation, 2896 South Broadway, Englewood, Colorado 80110.

across the chart, making the chart difficult to see. If a gooseneck or tensor lamp is available, place it in such a position (about a 45° angle) approximately 3 feet back to illuminate the wall chart. If a light meter is being used, the lighting should range between 10 and 30 foot candles. However, if electric equipment is used, the lighting is usually automatically provided and is sufficient.

ROOM SET-UP

Survey the room to be used for testing. Set up the equipment according to the electrical outlets provided. If using lighted equipment, try to facilitate a convenient flow of traffic. No one should pass through the testing area upon entering or exiting. When selecting a position for the charts, place them so that others waiting to be screened are not able to study the charts.

Make sure the power cords needed with electric equipment are not placed in a hazardous position. When testing, the position of the examiner and charts must be at eye level to those being screened. For example, when testing small children, assume a sitting position; with taller individuals, stand to be able to make good observations.

Whenever possible, have a small table close to the screener in order to record the tests results *immediately*. Do not try to remember the figures or findings. Place all of the various equipment within reach to ensure organized and proper screening. *Always make very sure that the individual being tested understands exactly what is expected of him or her before each test.*

PROCEDURES FOR TESTING CENTRAL VISUAL ACUITY

Materials

Necessary materials are a 10- or 20-foot "E" (or alphabet) chart, large block E and paper illustrated E (for small children), occluded glasses or Dixie cups, tape measure, masking tape, recording forms, pens, and, in some cases, additional lighting.

Technique

When screening the preschooler, either for a single unit or a multiphasic battery, preparation is the same. Approach the child as "playing a game." The child should not feel an apprehension of "being tested." Visual aids are a great asset. For example, a large wooden or plastic E when testing with a Snellen E chart makes the test a matching game. It is good also to have a large printed E so that the screener and the child being tested can practice before entering the screening area. When a child understands how to play the game, he or she is ready to be tested. If there are many children to test, one can easily teach a group of one to eight children how to play the game, having the whole group try it together, then individually. The tester uses the large printed E, moving it in the various directions with the children matching their block E's. For better comprehension, have a small E (20/30) on the back of the large printed E (20/200). The tester can also play the game with the child being screened. Introduce the large E first, followed by the small E, which will teach size association. Thus, when the child sees the chart with different sizes of E's he or she will be accustomed to the various sizes. All of the above tips will assist in gaining good accurate vision screening. It has been found through past experience that when working with preschoolers (ages 3 to 6) a higher performance level is obtained if the parents are not present. However, when screening groups of children, have three or four children come into the screening area at the same time, having the oldest go first to lead the way, and let the others observe how the game is played. Position the children to prevent their studying the chart before their turn. Bring the next group in while the last child of the previous group is being screened. This makes a nice smooth screening without time lapses. Finally, and most important, when screening, always be certain that the child understands what he or she is expected to do. If the child fails the screening, it is because he or she may have a vision problem, not because the child doesn't understand how to play the game. This will eliminate the number of over-referrals.

When testing preschoolers (especially 3- to 4-year-olds), place their heels on the tape where the footage has been marked. It is recommended to use the "isolated method," which is exposing only E at a time while the rest of the chart is concealed.

Hand the child the large toy E. Instruct him to *"match"* his E to the E shown on the chart. The child should feel no stress.

The full line exposure or linear testing may be used effectively with individuals who are over 7 years of age.

When an individual is wearing glasses, always test first with the glasses on, but be sure to note the condition of the glasses, making sure they are well fitting, clean, and clear of permanent scratches.

The single most important factor to know about an individual being tested is his or her *age.* An individual's visual acuity depends primarily on what he or she should see based on age (see Table 1).

Always test an individual down to the line he or she is expected to see regardless of how well he or she performs. There are always those individ-

Table 1.   Expected vision scale (based on age)

Age, years	Expected vision	Lines to test, feet
3 →	20/40	70, 50, 40
4 →	20/30	50, 40, 30
5 →	20/30	50, 40, 30
6 and above	20/20	40, 30, 20

uals who are reluctant or unsure of themselves at the beginning of a screening, but as they see how easy it is they increase their performance.

Format

An easy format to follow is given.

1. Begin the screening by testing both eyes first; then test the right eye, then the left eye.
2. When testing the eyes independently, use occluded glasses if they are provided or use a Dixie cup or construction paper cut in an oval shape having no sharp edges to occlude the eye. Some eye infections may be transmitted, therefore, discard the paper occluder after it has been used.
3. Test three lines of the chart.
4. The last line to be tested is that line which an individual should be able to see, based on his or her age (see Table 1).
5. Use an "S" pattern. That is, go back and forth across the chart, right to left. When moving along the chart the tester will know how many E's or letters have been presented.
6. Give four E's per line.
7. An individual should get more than half (three out of four) responses correct to be considered "passing the line"; if he or she does not, then the individual fails the line. Always test an individual to the line the person should be able to see.
8. The visual acuity is recorded as the lowest line on the chart, where an individual has given three out of four (or more than half) of the responses correctly.
9. Be sure to record the findings while completing each line, testing down the chart. Do not try to remember what an individual did for both eyes, right and left.

Recording Visual Acuity

The findings are usually recorded as a fraction or ratio. As an example, in the ratio 20/30, the first number (20) gives the distance (in feet) from the chart to the individual being tested, while the second number (30) indicates the line of letters that a person sees (the individual can see the 30-foot line of letters).

Suggested Criteria for Referral

The criteria for referring are usually set by the local school health committees, state or county health departments, or private physicians. One suggested method for accurate referrals is as follows:

1. Always refer an individual who has a two-line difference from expected vision (example: 20/20 (age 6 and above), refer 20/40).
2. Always refer an individual who has a two-line difference in acuity between the eyes (example: right eye 20/30, left eye 20/50). This could indicate a possible amblyopia (lazy eye) in a preschool-age child.
3. Always refer an individual with signs or symptoms that may indicate a problem, such as red rims, watering, squint, excessive rubbing, or complaints of headaches or nausea.

Always recheck at a later date before referring for a professional exam.

PROCEDURES FOR TESTING HYPEROPIA (Excessive Far-Sightedness)

When testing for hyperopia, a screener checks to see how well an individual can see up close (for example, the vision that is used when reading a book).

Materials

The materials needed are an E chart and a 2.5 lens.

Technique

1. Place the individual's heels on the marker.
2. Place the lens on the individual, allowing a few seconds for eye adjustment before commencing with testing.
3. Using both eyes, have the individual read the normal "expected vision" line (see "Expected Vision Scale").

Criteria for Referral

An individual that indicates *no* hyperopia problems will "blur out" and not be able to see the expected line clearly. When the expected line is read correctly (while wearing the lens), the individual may have a problem with hyperopia (excessive far-sightedness) and should be rechecked at a later date. Always recheck at a later date before referring for an eye exam.

PROCEDURES FOR TESTING FOR COLOR DEFICIENCIES

Materials

An Ishiara color plate, an improvised color chart, or a piece of electric equipment that has a color test included are needed. The six basic colors (red, white, black, yellow, blue, green), in the form of cubes or blocks, help in testing younger children.

Technique

Point out or light up one color and ask the individual being tested to identify the color. When testing young children, who may not know their colors, give the blocks that are being shown and ask him or her to match one of the colored blocks to the color square shown on the chart or wall. A preschooler need not know colors by verbal response, but merely by matching, therefore the examiner is not testing his or her vocabulary in identification but what the child sees.

If this system seems to fail, try painting the bottom of a muffin tin the six basic colors. Give the child the six cubes and ask him or her to put the cubes in the little cup that is the same color. It may sometimes be necessary to give the child a few minutes to complete the task. Another form of color testing is using muted strains of yarn; the tester needs the six basic colors, and five shades of each basic color. Put all the yarn into one box and ask a child if he would help divide or put the different colors of yarn into separate piles. Most research has proven that there is a necessity for testing only males for color blindness.

Criteria for Referral for Color Blindness

Testing for color blindness is probably valued more for its educational value than its visual value. If a person would fail the test by mixing the color responses, he or she should be rechecked with a more refined test (for example, the Ishiara test). When the color blindness areas have been identified, inform the individual in order to enable the person to compensate. The teacher should be notified of color blindness in order to modify teaching methods in using color-coded techniques.

PROCEDURES FOR TESTING MUSCLE IMBALANCE

Materials

There are several ways to effect this test. It would be too involved to list the materials that might be used for a variety of tests.

Techniques

In reference to testing for problems with muscle imbalance, it is important to see that there may be a relationship between how an individual tests for central vision acuity and muscle imbalance. If an individual has an imbalance in one eye and in testing his or her acuity the examiner finds that the eye is weaker than normal, it might be caused by the imbalance which may cause the eye to wander excessively rather than function normally. Sometimes the lack of use may cause a loss in vision. However, the reverse is also true. An individual may have an eye that has some imbalance, but when tested for problems in acuity the eye tests as normal. This would tend to indicate that, although the individual has an imbalance, he or she uses the vision in that eye and therefore has no immediate problem with imbalance. The degree that the eye wanders is not necessarily related to the severity of a muscle imbalance problem. It could depend on how much the eye is used. Therefore, when testing for muscle imbalance, the above information should be kept in mind. The following methods may be utilized in testing for a muscle imbalance.

A few machines on the market have muscle imbalance tests incorporated into their battery testing; for example, the Tetmus or Comtronic's multipurpose vision screener.

The cover-patch test is simply a test in which an individual stands directly in front of the tester who requests the person to fix or look at a specific object either on or behind the examiner. Take a Dixie cup or the hand of the child being tested, place in a cupped position, and have the child position it over one eye. In a constant rhythmic pattern cover and uncover the eye. Sometimes, if an eye is imbalanced, the eye will move either in or out, or up or down. What the tester is determining with this gross test is whether the eye is functioning or whether it is in a state of relaxation. After the Dixie cup or hand is removed from the eye, the eye will go back into place. If the individual is not keeping a fixed stare on an object and every time the tester uncovers the eye the individual is looking at something different, the test is not being accomplished. Try testing each eye separately.

In the reflection test, the individual is placed in front of the screener so that both are at eye level with each other. The examiner should have his or her back to direct sunlight. The sunlight will cross over the tester's shoulders into the eyes of the individual being tested. This helps to provide good reflection in the child's eyes. It is important to be certain that the individual's head is held straight. Carefully study where the white pin-dot of light reflection hits the child's eyes. If the light reflection is at exactly the same spot on both eyes, it indicates that the individual has no imbalance.

However, if one of the pin-dots is much lower than the other or one dot is in toward the nose while the other is out towards the temple, this could indicate the presence of a muscle imbalance.

Criteria for Referral

If an individual fails a test for muscle imbalance, a recheck should be made within a 3-week period. If the individual fails the recheck, determine what is the relationship between the acuity test and the muscle imbalance test. If the imbalance is so gross that it causes the cosmetic appearance of an individual to be remarkable, this could cause other types of problems later. Treatment and correction of muscle imbalances, such as eye exercises or surgery, are possible if done by a certain age.

POINTS TO REMEMBER

1. When testing an individual who wears glasses, first test with glasses.
2. The most important point that can be stressed in administering this battery of tests is making certain that the subject fully understands what he or she is expected to do.
3. Try to make the testing a pleasant experience both for the screener and the individual being tested.
4. When the subject requires rechecking, allow 3 to 4 weeks before retesting.

SUMMARY

The battery of tests that have been enumerated in the preceding pages are not the only screening tests that may be administered, but the above-mentioned tests seem to be those in which the largest percentage of problems will be identified. When doing a multiphasic vision screening, try to administer the tests in the order of their effectiveness. For example, the tester will find that there will be more problems with central visual acuity than another specific test; thus, start with that test. If one is following a sequence for testing, a child who might be a low performer will at least have received the most important test should he or she become too tired or refuse to continue the battery. When administering a battery of vision tests, be organized to facilitate smooth and effective screening. Always give the battery in the same sequence.

If one is using trained volunteers, it is most important to create an enthusiastic, educated, committed atmosphere. The attitude conveyed to volunteers will influence to a great deal the overall success of the program.

1. Volunteers must be given the feeling that they were *chosen* for the program because of their ability, and must be given responsibility for completing tasks.

2. Offer an in-service program, making it educational and worthwhile.

3. Do not put their commitment on a time basis.

4. Approach good workers with the philosophy that they will be involved in a beneficial program and that their time and talents are needed.

5. Teach them the tests and give the necessary training and responsibilities, and in turn expect their loyalties and solid support.

In developing good screening programs, there are ways to improve the system. Keep abreast of new techniques. Try to learn of the new equipment that is available.

Following completion of a program, take a look at the results, as it is through past results that one can build a better program in the future. Be critical and thorough in self-evaluation.

SUGGESTED READINGS

Crossed Eyes: A Needless Handicap. National Society for the Prevention of Blindness, Inc., New York.

Eye Inspection and Testing Visual Acuity of Preschool-Age Children. National Society for the Prevention of Blindness, Inc., New York.

Patz, A., and R. E. Hoover. 1969. Protection of Vision in Children. Charles C. Thomas, Publisher, Springfield, Ill.

Preschool Vision Screening. National Society for the Prevention of Blindness, Inc., New York.

Taubenhaus, L. J., and A. A. Jackson. 1969. Vision Screening of Preschool Children. Charles C. Thomas, Publisher, Springfield, Ill.

Vision Screening of Children. National Society for the Prevention of Blindness, Inc., New York.

Your Child's Sight. National Society for the Prevention of Blindness, Inc., New York.

VII
GUIDELINES FOR HEARING SCREENING OF THE INFANT, PRESCHOOL, AND SCHOOL-AGE CHILD*

Marion P. Downs, M.A.†

The purpose of these guidelines is to secure for all children their fundamental right to acquire the best language skills possible for them. The ultimate language ability of all deaf children is dependent, to a large degree, upon the age at which any deafness is identified. Therefore, early detection of the hearing loss is vital. Whether the habilitation of the deaf child involves auditory, oral, or manual language training, it will be most effective if begun in the first year of life.

This guide will delineate the procedures that are recommended in conducting a program of screening infants for hearing problems. It is proposed that these directions be utilized by the pediatrician, nurse, or otolaryngologist directing the program, with the consultation of a certified audiologist to help organize the program and to train the personnel who will conduct it.

The recommended program attacks the problem of identifying deafness in infants from three aspects: 1) the application of a simple Register of Infants at Risk for Deafness; 2) the conducting of audiological evaluations on the newborns on this list; 3) the follow-up screening of infants on

---

*The major portion of this chapter has been taken, with permission of the authors and publishers, from *Hearing in Children,* by J. A. Northern and M. P. Downs, The Williams & Wilkins Co., Baltimore, 1974.

†Associate Professor of Otolaryngology (Audiology), University of Colorado Medical Center, 4200 East Ninth Avenue, Denver, Colorado 80220.

the list at each office and clinic visit. This three-fold attack on congenital deafness will be described in detail in the following pages.

WHY SHOULD HEARING SCREENING PROGRAMS BE INSTITUTED FOR INFANTS?

THE PROBLEM

Forty-two thousand severely deaf children attend special schools or classes in the United States at the present time. At least 1 child in every 2,000 births is deaf or severely hard-of-hearing. In addition, 15 to 30 per 1,000 school children who attend regular school classes, numbering almost 500,000, have hearing loss of some degree (United States Health, Education and Welfare). The 560,000 children who will be born deaf or hard-of-hearing in the next 18 years are the target population for this guide.

Studies of children in schools for the deaf have shown that the primary handicap of these children is lack of adequate language skills (Templin, 1966). The language deficiency is not due to lack of dedicated teaching during the school years, but to the failure to institute language learning until after the age of 2, 3, 4, 5, or 6 years. Language acquisition has been shown to be a time-locked function, locked to early maturational periods in an infant's life. The longer language stimulation is delayed, the less efficient will be the language facility (Tervoort, 1964).

The existence of critical periods for language learning is postulated as the cause of language retardation in the deaf child just as it is for the experientially deprived child. Ths most crucial of the critical periods for language are thought to occur during the first 2 years of life, when the organism is biologically programmed for language learning (Edwards, 1968; Lenneberg, 1967; Tervoort, 1964). *It has been erroneously assumed that language could be introduced at 3, 4, or 5 years of age to the deaf child with completely successful results.* A great loss of manpower and of human satisfaction results from such assumptions.

Even a 1-month-old deaf infant can receive language input through a hearing aid if he has sufficient residual hearing, or through visual and manual language inputs if he is totally deaf (Downs, 1971). Placement in an appropriate therapy program is mandatory for the deaf infant just as soon as his problem is identified. Many centers throughout the country carry on active home-training programs for the deaf infant from birth to 3 years (American Speech and Hearing Association, 1973) and there is available a home correspondence course in auditory, visual, and manual language training procedures (Alpiner, 1971). This kind of early training will ensure for the deaf child the development of his potential language skills to their optimal level.

When one considers that there are 235,000 individuals in this country with severe hearing loss and a total number of over 8 million with bilateral hearing impairment of some degree (Health Information Series, 1971), both the economic implications of early training and the value in human happiness become staggering.

THE YIELD

The most ideal identification program will probably yield no more than 1 in 2,000 of the entire population (California State Department of Public Health and Public Health Service, Department of Health, Education and Welfare, 1971). Two factors are operating here: first, that no screening procedure can be expected to identify 100 percent of the affected individuals; and second, that many severe deafnesses occur at some time after birth in both the genetic or exogenous categories (Bergstrom, Hemenway, and Downs, 1971; Fraser, 1971). However, when a High Risk Register is used the yield becomes at least 1 in 100 (Stewart, 1973).

The fact that even inherited deafness can occur at some time after birth makes it necessary to screen vigilantly for hearing problems during all the early months and years of life.

The kind of program that is being recommended rests on the principle that most deafness will occur in those infants who are *at risk* for deafness. Actual figures from infant screening programs have found that 75 to 90 percent of the infants ultimately found to be deaf would have been listed on a High Risk Register (Bergstrom et al., 1971; California State Department of Public Health and Department of Health, Education and Welfare, 1971). Supposedly, the cases of deafness which would not be on a register are those caused by recessive deafness for which the family history is too remote to recall. A certain number of these cases may develop deafness at some time after birth rather than being born with the disorder (Fraser, 1971). The actual numbers of this type of deafness are not known.

The nurse may conduct both the screening tests and the application of the High Risk Register. If so, her duties specifically will be: 1) to conduct the oral or written interview of the mother; 2) to search the medical records for the high risk categories described; 3) to maintain a follow-up system of children listed in this register; 4) to conduct the hearing test; 5) to report the results.

HOW
SHOULD INFANT HEARING SCREENING BE DONE?

SCREENING FOR THE NEWBORN INFANT

There are two basic steps to follow in identifying deafness in the newborn infant: First, the application of the High Risk Register; and second, follow-up evaluations. These will be described in detail.

Application of the High Risk Register

The high risk categories that are recommended for a register are ones which have been culled from exhaustive lists. Although only a few categories are listed for inclusion in this program, it is recommended that all participants in a program should study the longer list and become familiar with all the syndromes associated with deafness (Bergstrom et al., 1971; Black et al., 1971; California State Department of Public Health, 1971). The simplified list that is given here is essentially that recommended by the National Joint Committee on Infant Screening.[1] It is this list that will yield at least 1 deaf child in 100 on the High Risk Register.[2] As a mnemonic aid, the categories can be remembered as the *"A, B, C, D,'s"* (Downs and Silver, 1972): *"A,"* *Affected family*—the presence of any form of sensorineural hearing loss (other than presbycusis, i.e., hearing loss that begins in old age) in a family member; *"B,"* *Serum bilirubin level greater than 15 mg/100 ml* in premature infants and 20 mg/100 ml in term newborns, or hyperbilirubinemia due to blood group incompatibility in the newborn period; *"C,"* *Congenital rubella syndrome*—rubella at any time during pregnancy (sometimes the hearing loss is the sole symptom); *"D,"* *Defects of the ears, nose, or throat*—a malformed, low set, or absent pinna; a cleft palate or lip (including submucous cleft); any residual abnormalities of the first arch; any other anatomic abnormality of the otorhinolaryngeal system; *"s,"* *Small at birth*—Infants weighing less than 1,500 grams at birth have an appreciably greater risk of having hearing defects.

Functionally, the high risk categories are divided into three sections: those identifiable by query of mothers, those identifiable by visual examination, and those identifiable by physical examination in medical records.

---

[1] Composed of representatives from the American Academy of Pediatrics, the American Academy of Ophthalmology and Otolaryngology, and the American Speech and Hearing Association.

[2] It has been found that 6 to 10 percent of the newborn population will be in the abbreviated list, depending on the type of hospital clientele.

Identification through Query of the Mother A written questionnaire (see Chart 1) should be administered (translations in Spanish and other languages should be made). This questionnaire should be given to all new mothers in the hospital at some time after the baby is born. It should be prefaced with an explanation that "We are conducting a survey of all the babies born in this hospital, to see how many families have certain hearing problems. We would appreciate your help in this survey. There is nothing to worry about if you answer 'yes' to any of the questions, so do the best you can with them."

Interview following the Questionnaire When the forms are collected, each should be looked at, and a brief confirmation obtained on the negative responses: "You don't know of anyone in your two families who couldn't hear well before they were older?" and "You had no illness during pregnancy?"

If there has been a "yes" answer to the first question, check on the three subquestions. The age of the beginning of the loss should be queried further: "Does this relative speak clearly and distinctly?"; "Did he always speak clearly?" (If he was never able to speak well, it is a sign that a profound hearing loss was present very early in life or at birth); "Did he go

Chart 1. Questionnaire to be administered to all new mothers in hospital

---

1. Do you know any one of the baby's relatives who couldn't hear well before they were 50 years of age? Think hard about all your family and your husband's family.

    YES_____ NO_____

    a. If NO, proceed to question 2.
    b. If YES, answer these questions:
        1. Who were they? (relationship to baby)

        _____

        2. How old are they now?

        _____

        3. How old were they when loss occurred?

        _____

2. Did you have a rash with fever during pregnancy?

    YES_____ NO_____

    At what time in your pregnancy?

    _____

    Did the doctor call it German measles?

    YES_____ NO_____

3. Do you have any reason to worry that your child may have a hearing loss?

    _____

to regular schools or to special schools?"; "Did he ever wear a hearing aid?"; "Did he ever have surgery for his ear problem?"; "When?" (surgery when young is an indication that the loss was caused by otitis media, which may not be inherited; surgery after 20 years of áge can point to otosclerosis, which is inherited).

The cause of the loss can be queried further: "Was the cause diagnosed and identified by a doctor?"; "What exactly did he say about it?"; "From whom did you get the information about the loss?" (if second or third-hand, the information may be faulty).

Oral Query   If writing is a problem for the mother, the same questionnaire can be administered orally to the mother and the answers recorded.

Identification through Visual Observations of the Infant

Cleft Lip or Palate   The cleft lip is an immediately observable malformation, but cleft palate, and particularly submucous clefts, should be searched for by a physician. Submucous cleft has been found to be associated with congenital middle-ear anomalies, so it is important that the palate be carefully examined.

A bifid uvula is always accompanied by submucous cleft, but the cleft may be present without this symptom. Palpation of the juncture between the soft and hard palate will reveal a notch in the bony part. Get the report on this examination from the physician.

Malformations of the Ears   These may be obvious, but they also may be very subtle. Atresia, with partial formation of the pinna or small tab of skin where the pinna should be, is easily observed. Often, however, the ears are merely low set, or they may not have complete formation of helix, antihelix, tragus, or antitragus. A small tab of skin may occur in front of the pinna, on the cheek, with an otherwise normal-looking ear. Sometimes these symptoms are accompanied by cranial malformations of the nose, eye orbits, maxilla, or cranial bones, so that any odd-looking feature may be a clue (Black et al., 1971).

Do not be misled if one ear looks perfectly normal and there is some abnormality of the other ear. The apparently normal ear does not necessarily have normal hearing; the incidence of congenital middle-ear anomalies in the "good" ears opposite malformed ones is extremely high.

Identification through Search of the Medical Records and Physical Examinations

Whoever is assigned to examine the mother's and infant's medical records must be well trained in interpreting doctors' abbreviations and terminology (as well as their handwriting). The following items should be searched for: 1) birth weight less than 1,500 grams; 2) bilirubin titer greater than 15 mg/100 ml depending on gestational age or if early transfusion of blood was given.

Follow-up Evaluations

It is recommended by the Joint Committee that all infants on the High Risk Register be given an audiological evaluation by 2 months of age. Where possible this should be done by a certified audiologist. However, procedure of follow-up that is mandatory is described in the next section.

Provision should be made to report to the managing physicians the names of the infants who have been placed in the "at risk for deafness" category. Follow-up of these infants can be made by the hospital screening program personnel or by the Public Health Agency, whichever is appropriate. In any case, the managing physicians or the well-baby clinic to which the child will be taken must be aware of their responsibility in screening the child further for hearing loss or referring to an agency that can do the screening, and then reporting this follow-up to the proper agency.

SCREENING FOR THE OLDER
INFANT IN OFFICE AND WELL-BABY CLINIC

The procedures recommended when the older infant is seen in well-baby clinic or doctor's office can be best remembered by the mnemonic "*H.E.A.R.*" (Downs and Silver, 1972).

"*H.*" *Hearing concern?* Is the mother concerned about the infant's hearing? Most mothers of deaf children have some suspicion of this by the time the child is 6 months old.

"*E.*" *Ear tests normal?* Does the infant respond normally to a simple orientation test using noisemakers? (See subsequent section on testing with one observer.)

"*A.*" *Awaken to sound?* Does the infant stir or awaken in response to noise when he is sleeping in a quiet room? If the mother has not observed such behavior, she should be asked to look for it and report at the next visit. Should she say that the infant responds to the slamming of doors or to other vibrations but not to the spoken voice or to other sounds, he may be responding only to the vibration caused by the forcible closing of the door and not to the sound. A specific question that the mother should be asked is "When he is sleeping quietly in his room and you come in and talk or make noises, does he stir or awaken from his sleep?" He need not do this every time, but a few reliable reports are all that is necessary. The reason for this question is that it gives mother a specific simple observation to make that is not concerned with slamming doors, stamping feet, or engine vibrations, all of which a deaf child will respond to.

"R." Responses in the developmental and communication scales? Are the child's prelinguistic and linguistic skills at the expected levels in the developmental and communication scales? Here it is recommended that some screening scales be given which identify developmental and communication lags as well as hearing status. The DDST, Bayley Scales, etc., are useful. In addition, a simplified questionnaire for various age levels will be described in Chart 2.

Testing with One Observer—A Simplified Procedure by Downs

Equipment and Environment A quiet room is required, with little distraction from the outside. The suggested list of equipment is the following:

Squeeze Toy A soft rubber squeeze toy should be selected that makes a breathy "whoosh" sound, not a throaty noise. When buying it, compare different ones and find the one that sounds the highest pitched and can be made to sound the softest.

Bell A small gold East India import bell produces the highest pitch and also the softest ring. Compare the bells and select the one that is highest and softest. We have measured the output of such bells and found that they produce only frequencies around 4,000 Hz when rung slightly, at levels as low as 30 dB sound pressure level.

Rattle The usual baby rattle is adequate, providing it can be handled to produce a soft rattling sound. One may often find a toy plastic block that has sandlike material in it, that produces a nice, sudden rustling sound.

If you survive the scrutiny of the toy store clerk after making these selections, you are in business as an infant tester.

One chair is needed, for the mother to sit in with the child on her lap. A colorful toy like a small doll should be available as a distraction, but it should not be too attractive or it will engage the whole attention of the child.

Procedure The tester kneels at a 45° angle to the side of the child, with the distracting toy in one hand and the noisemaker well hidden in the other. When the baby's attention is engaged by the toy held in front of him, she makes the sound in the hand held close to the floor, out of the peripheral vision of the child. If an orientation response is seen after one or two presentations, the tester kneels on the other side and uses another noisemaker to test on that side. The tester will learn by experience that for the 0- to 4-month age level the sound must be produced quite loudly, but at 6 to 9 months it can be produced more softly and by 10 to 12 months it should be made as soft as possible.

The expected response is some sort of head turn toward the sound. An exact description of the head turn and accompanying eye movement should be noted. The expected responses at each age level are as follows:

0 to 4 months   Eye widening, eye blink (in a very quiet environment) or arousal from sleep as in newborn testing.

4 to 7 months   By 4 months, a "rudimentary" head turn is seen: a "wobble" of the head even slightly toward the sound:

This response gradually matures until at 6 months the head turn is definite, toward the side of the sound, but only on a plane level with the eyes. The infant does not fixate the sound source in the lower level where it comes from:

By 7 months there is an inclination to find the sound source on the lower level; the child will look first to the side and then down:

He may even be mature enough to find the source directly:

7 to 9 months   At the beginning of this period he should soon find the sound source on the lower level directly, but if the sound is presented on a level above his head he will only look toward the side. At the end of this period he may begin to look toward the side and then up, to fixate the higher sound source:

9 to 13 months   At 9 months, the beginning indirect localization on the higher level will be seen which soon turns to direct localization:

We thus see shortly after 1 year of age a direction localization of sounds in any plane:

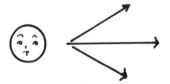

13 to 24 months The same type of orientation prevails for the older child as was seen for the 13-month-old. In other words, the full maturation of the auditory behavior of the child occurs at about 13 months and does not change significantly after that.

Interpreting Test Results In making the observations described above we are looking for more than a hearing loss. The hearing loss will be

Chart 2. Questions to ask the mother at the well-baby examination

2 months			
Hearing	1. Have you had any worry about your child's hearing?	YES____	NO____
	2. When he's sleeping in a quiet room, does he move and begin to wake up when there's a loud sound?	YES____	NO____
Developmental and Communication	3. Does he lift up his head when he's lying on his stomach?	YES____	NO____
	4. Does he smile at you when you smile at him?	YES____	NO____
	5. Does he move both hands together in the same way?	YES____	NO____
	6. Does he look at your face without your making gestures at him?	YES____	NO____
4 months			
Hearing	1. Have you had any worry about your child's hearing?	YES____	NO____
	2. When he's sleeping in a quiet room, does he move and begin to wake up when there's a loud sound?	YES____	NO____
	3. Does he try to turn his head toward an interesting sound, or when his name is called?	YES____	NO____

Continued

Chart 2.—*Continued*

---

4 months

Developmental and Communication

4. Does he lift his head up to 90° and look straight ahead? YES____ NO____
5. Does he touch his hands together and play with them? YES____ NO____
6. Does he laugh and giggle without being tickled or touched? YES ____ NO____
7. Does he coo to himself and make noises when he's alone? YES____ NO____

---

6 months

Hearing

1. Have you had any worry about your child's hearing? YES____ NO____
2. When he's sleeping in a quiet room, does he move and begin to wake up when there's a loud sound? YES____ NO____
3. Does he turn his head toward an interesting sound or when his name is called? YES____ NO____

Developmental and Communication

4. Does he lift up his head and chest with his arms? YES____ NO____
5. Does he keep his head steady when sitting? YES____ NO____
6. Does he roll over in his crib? YES____ NO____
7. Does he reach for objects within his reach and hold them? YES____ NO____
8. Does he see small objects like peas or raisins? YES____ NO____

---

8 months

Hearing

1. Have you had any worry about your child's hearing? YES____ NO____
2. When he's sleeping in a quiet room, does he move and begin to wake up when there's a loud sound? YES____ NO____
3. Does he turn his head directly toward an interesting sound or when his name is called? YES____ NO____
4. Does he enjoy ringing a bell or shaking a rattle? YES____ NO____

Developmental and Communication

5. Does he support most of his weight on his legs? YES____ NO____
6. Can he sit alone uaided for 5 minutes? YES____ NO____
7. Can he sit and look for objects that have fallen out of sight? YES____ NO____
8. Can he pick up two objects, one in each hand? YES____ NO____

Continued

Chart 2.—*Continued*

8 months

Developmental and Communication	9.	Can he transfer an object from one hand to the other? YES____ NO____
	10.	Can he feed himself a cracker? YES____ NO____
	11.	Does he make a number of different sounds and change their pitch? YES____ NO____
	12.	Does he clap his hands in imitation and make noises at the same time? YES____ NO____

10 months

Hearing	1.	Have you had any worry about your child's hearing? YES____ NO____
	2.	When he's sleeping in a quiet room, does he move and begin to wake up when there's a loud sound? YES____ NO____
	3.	Does he turn his head directly toward an interesting sound or when his name is called? YES____ NO____
	4.	Does he try to imitate you if you make his own sounds? YES____ NO____
	5.	Does he play "peek-a-boo" with you? YES____ NO____
Developmental and Communication	6.	Can he stand for at least 5 seconds, holding onto crib or chair? YES____ NO____
	7.	Does he try to hold onto a toy when it's pulled away? YES____ NO____
	8.	Is he shy or afraid of strangers? YES____ NO____
	9.	Can he pull himself to standing position alone? YES____ NO____

12 months

Hearing	1.	Have you had any worry about your child's hearing? YES____ NO____
	2.	When he's sleeping in a quiet room, does he move and begin to wake up when there's a loud sound? YES____ NO____
	3.	Does he turn his head directly toward an interesting sound or when his name is called? YES____ NO____
	4.	Is he beginning to repeat some of the sounds that you make? YES____ NO____
Developmental and Communication	5.	Can he pick up a raisin or pea? YES____ NO____
	6.	Can he get to a sitting position without help? YES____ NO____
	7.	Does he wave "bye-bye" or "pat-a-cake" when you tell him to? YES____ NO____
	8.	Can he say "mama" or "dada"? YES____ NO____

suspected if the child does not respond appropriately on either side, or if he orients to the wrong side. But, there are other conclusions that can be drawn from the type of orientation he displays. The direction of the baby's orientation must be within the criterion levels described above if he is to be cleared. Take, for example, a 1-year-old child who is able to turn his head only on a lateral plane, level with his eyes, even though the sound source is below or above that level. Such a child should be referred for developmental evaluation, for he is certainly at risk for retardation or for central problems. He should be showing auditory behavior commensurate with the normative value for his age. Any long-standing problem should be referred for in-depth testing of status of developmental communicative skills.

Follow-up

The ideal referral for children who do not pass the screening at office or clinic visit is to an otoaudiologic center, a center where an otologist can examine the child's ears and an audiologist can test the child's hearing in a standard sound room. Even if the high risk children are passed at their office or clinic visit, they should continue to be screened at every succeeding visit, for the danger of developing a hearing loss in these children is never past.

The exception is the infants in the high bilirubin category and those in the small birth weight category. Once a professional has determined to his satisfaction that there is perfectly normal hearing in such a child at 3, 6, or 9 months, there is no reason to recheck the hearing regularly, other than is done for non-high risk children.

Hearing, Development, and Communication Questionnaire (Chart 2) The mother can be asked the questions, graded to various age levels, that are given in Chart 2. The application of such a two-part questionnaire is necessary to distinguish the hearing questions from those related to general development.

Another characteristic of the deaf infant is that he is unusually visually alert, and attends to movement in his peripheral vision. Therefore, if the mother reports that he turns around to an interesting sound or when his name is called, the question must be asked if she is sure that the sound is out of his peripheral visual field.

One of the erroneous assumptions that have been made in the past is that a deaf infant does not babble or make sounds like a normal hearing infant. Nothing could be further from the truth. *Until the age of 6 months, the deaf infant sounds exactly like the normal infant; he babbles just as much; he increases his vocalizations* when the parent appears and coos at him just as the normal child; and only an expert phonetician could identify the subtle qualitative differences in the babbling sounds that the deaf child makes. Therefore, great care has been taken in the questionnaire not to assume that the baby's vocalizations are any index of his ability to hear.

A very misleading indication is a mother's report that her baby says "mama" at around the age of 1 year, and that therefore the baby must be hearing at that point. Oddly enough, the mothers of most deaf children have made just such a report, and it is universally true that a profoundly deaf infant will appear to be saying "mama" at around 1 year of age. Actually what he is saying is "amah," which is the most primitive sound that can be made, involving as it does the almost animal-like "ah" vocalization plus the coming together of the lips. It has been postulated that one of the reasons for its development is that in infancy the baby is carried close to the mother, and feels the vibrations or hears low frequencies of his mother's voice, and is thus stimulated to perpetuate the sounds. At any rate, the sounds soon drop off, and nothing remains but the "ah" vocalization in a strident voice.

It is certainly true that in the process of brief clinic visits it is sometimes impossible to observe spontaneous vocalizations. If there are concerns it is strongly advised to attempt to elicit this behavior rather than accept a report from the accompanying adult, especially when it is in doubt.

WHY
SHOULD HEARING SCREENING PROGRAMS BE CONDUCTED FOR YOUNG CHILDREN?

SCREENING FOR THE PRESCHOOL AND SCHOOL-AGE CHILD

It is vital to the child's cognitive development that he hear well during these early years of life. Mild to moderate hearing loss may not have been identified during the first 2 years of life, and now is the time to look for it.

Studies have shown that even mild hearing losses can cause learning problems (Bond, 1935; Downs, 1975; Ling, 1959; Holm and Kunze, 1969; Luke, 1965; Scottish Council, 1956). These losses are of a kind that are due to otitis media. Ninety percent of the hearing losses of children who reach school age are caused by otitis media, and can be remedied medically or surgically. Long before school age is reached these problems should be identified.

A small number of sensorineural losses will not have been discovered during the first 2 years of life. These may only number about 10 percent of all the hearing problems in children, but they are important to identify because of the severity of the handicaps they cause. Two screening tools are presently available to nurses: pure tone screening audiometry and pneumatic otoscopy. These will be described in detail.

Guidelines for Pure Tone Hearing Screening of the Young Child

Any agency that attracts preschoolers in large numbers to its doors should undertake a hearing screening program. These agencies include: 1) doctors' offices; 2) public well-baby clinics; 3) neighborhood health centers; 4) Headstart programs; 5) public school preschool programs; 6) child care centers.

Pure Tone Screening Tests for the 2- to 3-Year-Old

1. Selection of a quiet room for the testing should be made carefully, keeping in mind the building noises and the traffic in the area. (Ideal screening conditions call for commercial sound-treated booths, but realistically most clinics cannot afford this purchase.)

2. Check the hearing of your own ear or that of another person whose hearing has been previously tested and is known to be normal. If those thresholds have not changed more than 5 dB, the instrument should be in good calibration.

3. Play-conditioning procedure for testing the 3- and 4-year-old child includes the following:

   a. Have available a pegboard, a ring tower, plain blocks, or other simple toy that is motivating to young children.

   b. With headphones on your ears, take a block (or peg, etc.) and hold it up to one ear as if listening. Make believe you hear a sound, say: "I hear it," and put the block on the table.

   c. Put the phones on the child's ear and hold his hand with the block up to his ear.

   d. Sound a 50-dB[3] tone at 1000 Hz and guide his hand to build the block tower. Repeat once or twice and then see if he can do it alone. If he can, go on.

   e. Set the hearing level at 25 dB and repeat the test. Sweep through the other frequencies (1,000, 2,000, and 4,000 Hz).

---

[3] All hearing levels are in American National Standards Institute (ANSI) calibration levels. This means that the audiometer should be calibrated to the levels recommended by the ANSI and should be so noted on the audiometer.

f. Rescreen any child who fails to respond at any one frequency in either ear.

g. Refer for threshold audiogram the child who still fails to respond at even one frequency.

Pure Tone Screening Tests for the Mature 4-Year-Old Child and the 5-Year-Old Child

1. Instruct the child that he is going to hear some little tones or "beeps," and every time he hears one he is to raise his hand.

2. Set the hearing level dial to 50 dB and give him a practice tone of 1,000 Hz. If he responds with handraising, proceed to No. 3.

3. Set the hearing level of screening audiometer at 25 dB.

4. Screen one student at a time, at 1,000, 2,000, and 4,000. Sweep-check each student.

5. At the completion of testing the group, rescreen any who fail to respond to the tone at the level of 25 dB at any frequency.

6. Refer for threshold audiogram all those who still fail to respond to one frequency in either ear.

Pure Tone Hearing Screening of the School-age Child The health department or medical directors of all school systems, whether public, private, or parochial, should provide ongoing screening programs. Because good hearing is essential to the child's socioeducational development, the following benefits accrue from a well planned screening program: 1) *the prevention of handicapping hearing losses* through medical treatment which can be instituted when a child's ear problem is identified at an early age; 2) *the maintenance of adequate hearing for the child in the classroom* (many hearing impairments that affect the child's class work may go unnoticed unless a testing program detects them; medical treatment may be effective in 90 percent of the children found to have hearing problems); 3) *habilitation for those children with permanent hearing losses* that are identified by the screening program. Audiological, educational, and therapeutic approaches will help these children to function better in the classroom. Such children should be followed with monitoring audiometry and regular otological examinations.

Frequency of Testing Testing should be conducted annually in grades: kindergarten, 1,3,5, and 7. Annual tests should also be conducted on all transfers into the school system (including high school level students), and on all students with a history of previous hearing problems or familial history, until, following treatment, no decline in hearing is shown for three successive years.

Procedures

Environment Selection of a quiet room for the testing should be made carefully, keeping in mind the class schedules and the traffic that occurs on any given day. (Ideal screening conditions call for commercial sound-treated booths but, realistically, most schools cannot afford this purchase.)

The Individual Pure Tone Sweep-check Test This is the standard screening technique which should always be employed, even if other tests are to be used as supplements. 1) Set the hearing level of screening audiometer at 25 dB (ANSI). 2) Screen one student at a time at 1,000, 2,000, and 4,000. Sweep-check each student, using the handraising technique described for preschoolers. 3) At the completion of testing the group, rescreen any who fail to respond to the tone at any frequency in either ear. If a failure is obtained on the second screen, the child is considered to fail the test, and should be referred for threshold audiogram.

Follow-up Procedures after the Pure Tone Threshold Tests Otologic examination is scheduled for those children whose follow-up threshold audiometric test results show: 1) a hearing level of 25 dB (ANSI) or worse at any one frequency in the range of 250 to 2,000 Hz; 2) a hearing level of 35 dB (ANSI) or worse at any one frequency in the range of 4,000 to 8,000 Hz; 3) an air-bone gap of 15 dB or more in the 250 to 500 Hz range; 10 dB or more at 1,000 Hz.

Those experienced in hearing conversation programs agree that some over-referral to otological phases of the program is better than under-referral. Where there is a period of time between threshold testing and otological examination, experience has shown that about 12 percent of the children referred for otological examination will be found to be otologically normal. This percentage probably represents the spontaneous recovery of temporary ear conditions as well as some testing errors. However, the 12 percent figure may be used for a rough evaluation of the conditions under which testing is done, and the criteria which are used for referral for otological examination. If all children at otological examination show abnormalities, the program is probably missing some significant ear conditions that it is capable of identifying. If there are large numbers of otologically normal children referred, then valuable professional time is being used nonproductively.

Further Consultant Services These are given those children who are found to have irremediable hearing losses even after medical treatment has been concluded. These services include further audiological studies which may indicate need for: 1) hearing aid use; 2) special seating in classrooms; 3) classes for lip reading and auditory training; 4) referral to special schools or classes; 5) family consultation if or when it is deemed necessary.

Equipment and Environment At the present time, from the stand-point of their relative versatility, cost, and maintenance, the use of portable audiometers is recommended for school screening programs.

Concurrent with the purchase of any audiometric equipment there must be a plan to provide proper and periodic calibration and maintenance for the equipment. The reliability of an audiometer depends upon the accuracy of its setting, and no audiometer will indefinitely maintain the accuracy of its calibration. As a minimum, each audiometer should be calibrated yearly, or when the self-check shows any deviation. Even new audiometers should be self-checked for calibration accuracy before they are put into use.

Arrangements for periodic calibration and repair service should be made with a laboratory which is equipped to provide calibration to the standards of ANSI. The firm manufacturing the audiometer may provide or suggest calibration services. Larger universities or acoustic laboratories may have such facilities. Some laboratories and companies now provide calibration and maintenance services on a contract basis.

The yield of significant ear conditions and hearing losses is influenced greatly by the audiometric testing conditions. Ideal screening conditions call for commercial prefabricated sound-treated booths. Schools having continuing hearing conservation programs have been urged to provide such booths in school buildings. At the present time most school buildings do not have ideal conditions for audiometric screening.

The quietest room in the school building should be selected for audiometric screening. The room should be as far as possible from heating and other mechanical equipment, shops, music and typing rooms, and other sections where student traffic or scheduled activities create noise. The worst noises are steady or continuous such as those created by traffic or heating and ventilating equipment.

Pneumatic Otoscopic Examination

Many children may have hearing for pure tones that is within normal range, yet have ear disease that is otologically significant (Jordan and Eagles, 1961). Serous otitis media is the most common of such disease states. The only method of detecting such problems is through direct examination of the ear drum by pneumatic otoscopy.

In order for nurses to perform this examination they must be thoroughly trained by otolaryngologists who are willing to do the training and to give some supervision of the program. After the nurse has been trained, a validation check by the physician should be done on his or her findings on a number of children. This check will determine his or her accuracy in identifying ear disease. Such conditions as perforations, serous otitis, monomeric membranes, and scarred drums can be identified by this examination. Such cases should be referred for further evaluation by an otolaryngologist, even if normal hearing range prevails.

In summary, all of the guidelines explained in these chapters can easily be incorporated into useful knowledge for all nurses. Public health nurses or community nurses are in an enviable position to implement the recommendations mentioned. By very early identification and knowledgeable anticipatory guidance they can alleviate much unnecessary concern, not only physical-emotional but financial as well.

LITERATURE CITED

Alpiner, J. 1971. Personal correspondence. University of Denver, Speech and Hearing Clinic.

American Speech and Hearing Association (ASHA). 1973. A Guide to Clinical Services in Speech Pathology and Audiology, Washington, D.C.

Bergstrom, L., W. G. Hemenway, and M. P. Downs. 1971. A high risk registry to find congenital deafness. Otolaryngol. Clin. N. Amer. 4: 369–399.

Black, F. O., L. Bergstrom, M. P. Downs, and W. G. Hemenway. 1971. Congenital Deafness: A New Approach to Early Detection Through a High Risk Register. Associated University Press, Boulder, Colo.

Bond, G. L. 1935. Auditory and Speech Characteristics of Poor Readers. Teachers' Contribution to Education No. 657. Teachers College, Columbia University, New York.

California State Department of Public Health and Public Health Service. California Conference on Newborn Hearing Screening. Department of Health, Education and Welfare. 1971.

Downs, M. P. 1971. Audiological evaluation of the congenitally deaf infant. Otolaryngol. Clin. N. Amer. 4: 347–358.

Downs, M. P. 1975. Hearing Loss: Definition, Epidemiology and Prevention. Public Health Reviews, Israel.

Downs, M. P., and H. K. Silver. 1972. The A.B.C.D.'s to H.E.A.R.: Early identification in nursery, office and clinic of the infant who is deaf. Clin. Pediat. 11: 563–566.

Edwards, E. P. 1968. Kindergarten is too late. Sat. Rev. 60–79.

Fraser, G. R. 1971. The genetics of congenital deafness. Otolaryngol. Clin. N. Amer. 4: 227–247.

Health Information Series No. 140. 1971. Public Health Service Publication No. 1646, Department of Health, Education and Welfare, U.S. Government Printing Office, Washington, D.C.

Holm, V. A., and L. H. Kunze. 1969. Effect of chronic otitis media on language and speech development. Pediatrics 43: 833–839.

Jordan, R. E., and E. L. Eagles. 1961. The relation of air conduction audiometry to otologic abnormalities. Ann. Otol. Rhinol. Laryngol. 70: 819–827.

Lenneberg, E. H. 1967. Biological Foundations of Language. John Wiley & Sons, New York.

Ling, D. 1959. The education and general background of children with defective hearing. Unpublished research associateship thesis, Cambridge University, Institute of Education, 1959.

Luke, J. 1965. A comparative investigation of language abilities among children with limited auditory impairment. Master's thesis, Colorado State University, Ft. Collins.

Scottish Council for Research in Education. 1956. Hearing Defects in School Children. University of London Press, London.

Stewart, J. M. 1973. Genetic counseling. In J. Clausen, M. Flook, B. Ford, M. Green, and E. Popiel (eds.), Maternity Nursing Today. McGraw-Hill, New York.

Templin, M. 1966. Vocabulary problems of the deaf child. Int. Audiol. 5: 349.

Tervoort, B. 1964. Development of languages and the critical period. The young deaf child: Identification and management. Acta Otolaryngol. (Suppl.) 206: 247–251.

U.S. Department of Health, Education and Welfare, National Institutes of Health, Public Health Service. 1968. Grant No. NB07612, Human Communication and Its Disorders–an Overview. A report by the Sub-Committee on Human Communication and Its Disorders. U.S. Government Printing Office, Washington, D.C.

VIII
SPEECH AND LANGUAGE DEVELOPMENT

Kathleen Bryant, M.A. *

The development of speech and language is part of the normal growth pattern of a child. To be human is to communicate. The birth cry is the baby's announcement that he is here, and his ability to communicate increases with advancing age. The growth of his communication is like that of physical growth, proceeding in an orderly manner which may vary in rate, but which progresses in a predetermined fashion. Like all growth, if the developmental pattern is interrupted, problems may result.

Spoken language is a logical system by which one person communicates ideas and feelings to another person. It is not a solitary activity except during the early months of life. Vocalization, which occurs with the infant's first breath, sets off immediate verbal responses from the parental figures in his environment. Environmental reactions continue to produce reciprocal responses in the child until eventually language develops. Two basic sound patterns, which may be described as "comfort and discomfort" sounds, evoke responses in both child and mother in such a manner as to develop reciprocal communication. When a mother's voice is reassuring, the response will be a sigh of relief; when her voice is tense, the response will be screaming. Not only do "comfort and discomfort" sounds trigger a response, but they are used by the infant to express his feelings. A series of nasalized cries indicate hunger, which is immediately recognized by the mother, who responds by talking with her baby. When satisfied, the noises change to soft, cooing-like sounds which further stimulate adult conversation. Mother may reflect an interpretation of the baby's feeling state, whether it is one of content or discontent. Because sounds constantly stimulate responses from the people in the environment, the baby rapidly learns that noises can be used effectively to control his world.

*Senior Instructor, Department of Physical Medicine and Rehabilitation, University of Colorado School of Medicine, 4200 East 9th Avenue, Denver, Colorado 80220.

Speech is a motor act that requires precise integration of complex neuromuscular activity. The motor activity is not necessarily synonymous with language. Only when the speech sounds acquire meaning can they be referred to as language. Language develops independent of the motor skills necessary for articulation. It is a complex activity using sensory information that is received through visual, auditory, haptic, and kinesthetic modalities. Information is coded, stored, and eventually expressed as language. When interference occurs with the functioning or development of a single modality or any combination of the modalities concerned, there is a risk that language function, receptive and expressive, will be disturbed. It is too late to wait until a child "matures" to diagnose a speech or language problem. The patterns developed by the time the child is school age are frequently irreversible.

There are signs which can be noted at regular check-up clinic visits that indicate slow and/or deviant development. This does not mean the child will have a speech and language problem, but that he should be considered "at risk" and be carefully observed. Among the functions that should be carefully checked are the following.

HEARING

The importance of hearing to language, although discussed in a previous chapter, needs additional emphasis. Intact hearing is essential to the acquisition of spoken language. Ear infections, chronic colds, and, at times, allergies interfere with communication during critical periods for listening and may delay language development. Recent studies show that children with chronic otitis media are from 1 to 2 years behind their peers in language development. Hearing loss may also interfere with articulation patterns. A temporary hearing loss at the time a new sound is being learned affects the child's own "feedback" system and may result in a distorted production. Thus, an erroneous articulation pattern is learned. Neuromuscular activity becomes "set" or habitually responsive to the incorrect or distorted information received.

SUCKING

Sucking is a neuromuscular activity that is essential for survival. Experience with sucking and swallowing enables the infant to learn movements that are essential for articulation. Normal sucking involves the bringing of the lips together while pressing the tip of the tongue against the gum ridge. This forces the liquid back in the mouth so that the soft palate elevates and normal swallowing occurs. If the tongue tip is placed on the lower gum ridge in such a manner that its surface elevates to produce sucking, it can lead to the faulty "tongue thrust" pattern of swallowing with associated orthodontic problems.

HYPOTONICITY

Infant hypotonicity can signal "high risk" for speech problems. If large muscles are hypotonic, the fine muscles usually will be seriously involved. Oral muscle incoordination becomes apparent when a child is ready to eat solid food. Poor swallowing patterns cause food to be thrust out of the mouth. The child may actively bite food but be unable to chew. Failure to develop chewing patterns may cause mother to resort to the use of semiliquid foods, thus postponing speech learning. Fine motor control must develop before solid food is moved in the mouth and rotary jaw movements initiated for chewing. There are techniques for training a child to chew and swallow correctly. Children who fail to develop adequate articulation often have a history of long bottle feeding, refusal to eat solid foods, and difficulty with swallowing. Early detection and intervention can prevent future problems.

BREATHING

Breathing is an automatic neuromuscular activity that is necessary for survival. It is one of the most complex action patterns performed by man. It sustains life. It further sustains and regulates activity of the central nervous system. Correct breathing patterns are requisite to normal swift speech. When breathing patterns are abnormal, the volume, rhythm, and fluency of speech are disturbed. Incorrect breathing frequently causes a "flared" rib cage. Children who are labeled "reverse" breathers tend to make vocalizations on inhalation rather than on exhalation. Such abnormal breathing patterns continued through the early years may cause a child to be vulnerable to speech disorders. Early detection of breathing abnormalities is possible many months before words are spoken. The manner in which a child cries, laughs, babbles, and coos can provide information about the development of breathing.

A "quiet" baby may be suspect for poor breathing and/or poor muscular control, provided hearing is normal. By 3 months of age a normal baby develops a repertoire of sounds that are "understood" by his mother. She recognizes by his cries when he is hungry, tired, angry, or happy. If asked, she can describe the mood expressed by his "noises." She does not have to see his face to interpret his wishes. If a mother cannot give a description of her child's vocalizations, then more careful scrutiny should be made of his level of functioning.

VOCALIZING

Vocalizations are prespeech patterns which are modified through the use of facial muscles and body movements. Vocal play changes to recognizable phonetic sounds as the baby develops. All of the sounds later incorporated into speech are first heard in vocal play. If recognizable sounds do not appear, the possibility of deafness, delayed fine motor development, or retardation should be investigated. If the possibility of a hearing defect is eliminated, then careful evaluation of fine motor development should be made. Frequently, if gross motor milestones are present, fine motor activities may mistakenly be assumed to be adequate. For example, at about 4 months of age, a baby should turn over to a prone position. As he experiments with body movement, he raises his head, his tongue elevates, and he changes his throaty sounds to forward sounds. Fine motor development of the muscles used in articulation occurs by transition from nipple to spoon, from liquid to solid foods, and by the attempts to raise the head from the prone position. Mothers should be given all possible help to develop correct oral motor patterns in their infants. It is more economical than changing pathological behavior at a later age. Refinement of oral-pharyngeal movements, based on normal development, does not guarantee good articulation, but it does decrease the probability of severe speech defects.

RECEPTIVE LANGUAGE

The mode a baby uses to express his feelings is primitive. Before the baby can "express" his thoughts verbally, he has a long apprenticeship as a listener. To acquire language, not only the peripheral hearing mechanism must be intact, but the pathways in the central nervous system that transmit the message to the cortex must also be intact. Hearing is never turned off. The auditory mechanism receives sounds and interprets the environment 24 hours a day. Reception of sound does not necessarily assure beginning development of language. Listening or paying attention to the sounds received leads only to recognition of the sound pattern. Mother calls to baby, "I am coming" or "Wait until I finish the ironing." As these patterns are recognized, the child's responses will differ accordingly, indicating that he has recognized and interpreted the sound patterns.

Receptive language is measured by observing a child's responses to auditory stimuli. If appropriate responses are not observed but hearing is normal, central nervous system dysfunction may be present, or environmental circumstances may cause the apparent developmental lag. It is possible that ear infections and/or colds during critical periods for listening limit experience with language. Attempts to communicate may have been ignored, or the mother may have been *too* attentive and thus stifled attempts to communicate.

EXPRESSIVE LANGUAGE

Expressive language develops concurrently with receptive language. Initially the babbling is nondirected. All early vocalizations are self-stimulated. Therefore, mothers of deaf children frequently insist that the infant hears because he vocalizes. Nondirected vocalization should not be construed as expressive language. Between 6 and 8 months of age the rhythm and sounds of the native language are incorporated into the infant's babblings. This stage of development signals the learning of language. The use of appropriate rhythm and inflections enables people around the infant to interpret vocalizations. Between 10 and 12 months of age, one or two words are used meaningfully. The infant uses one word to express many desires. For example, it is by the rhythm and inflection that the mother interprets "go." The word may mean "I want to go outside," "I want to go with you," or "I want to use the toilet." By 18 months a vocabulary of 10 to 12 words including the possessive case should be observed. During the next 6 months expressive language increases at a phenomenal rate. By 2 years of age, the average child has a vocabulary of about 240 words. Substitution of words for gestures and acting out is established, and there is no longer any need to point or "to climb to the top shelf." A child can say, "I want the cookie up there." Long conversations with toys may be heard because little effort is made to inhibit the flow of language. By 3.5 years, he uses language to express fantasy and imagination and to test reality. Language at this time has almost replaced primitive manipulative behavior and enables him to establish self-regulation. As the child attempts to modify his environment by language, so his behavior is modified by the language of the people who surround him.

Critical periods for developing the motor aspects of speech, for identifying environmental sounds, for understanding language, and finally for the use or oral language occur during the first 3 years of life (Table 1). When acquisition of language is delayed, secondary problems should be

Table 1. Speech and language milestones: Observe these when the child is evaluated[a]

Age	Receptive language	Expressive language
Birth to 3 mos.	1. Is quieted by voice.[a] 2. Reacts to sudden noises. The response may be eye blink, beginning of head turn. 3. Responds to social gestures by smiling.	1. Strong cry.[a] 2. Vocalization of discomfort or comfort sounds. 3. Pre-babbling; the sounds are reflective.
3 to 6 mos.	1. Recognizes words such as "no, bye-bye, daddy," etc.[a] 2. Turns when a voice is heard without other stimulation. 3. Locates the source of sounds. 4. Responds appropriately to friendly and/or angry tones. 5. Responds to his own name.	1. Initiates vocal play.[a] 2. Laughs aloud. 3. Babbles, using a series of syllables on one breath. 4. Spontaneous smile in response to verbal play. 5. Vocalizes to self in mirror and to toys. 6. Expresses displeasure. 7. Experiments with his own voice.
6 to 9 mos.	1. Activity stops when he hears "no-no."[a] 2. Responds by raising his arms in response to "come up." 3. Shows recognition of family name. 4. Will sustain interest in pictures when a person names them.	1. Develops the sounds of his mother tongue.[a] 2. Combines several vowel sounds. 3. Responds to conversation by vocalizing. 4. Uses nonspecific "mama" and "dada" during babbling. 5. Initiates sounds such as a cough, tongue click, or kiss. 6. Develops rhythm.
9 to 12 mos.	1. Obeys simple instructions.[a] 2. Understands gestures. 3. Shows general under-	1. By first birthday, has one true word.[a] 2. Says "Mama" or "Dada" specifically.

Continued

Table 1.—*Continued*

Age	Receptive language	Expressive language
	standing of the meaning of simple statements and questions. 4. Waves "bye-bye" in response to verbal request. 5. Shows interest in speech over a long period of time.	3. Uses gestures with vocalization. 4. Spontaneously tries to imitate adult sounds. 5. Plays "peek-a-boo."
12 to 15 mos.	1. Plays game of "fetching" for his mother. 2. Pats a picture in a book. 3. Increased interest in names. 4. Listens to short nursery rhymes. 5. Shows understanding of new words.	1. Indicates his wants by vocalizing and pointing.[a] 2. Says three or four words appropriately including names. 3. Uses a flow of connected sounds that have inflection and that seem like a sentence.
15 to 18 mos.	1. Carries out two consecutive commands and/or directions.[a] 2. Can point to body parts on a doll. 3. Learns new words by association.	1. Uses 10 words including names. 2. Makes requests by naming objects. 3. Begins to repeat words he hears in adult conversation. 4. Leaves off the beginning and end of phrases, e.g., "see you later" becomes i/u/ler. 5. On one word responses he omits the final consonant.
18 to 24 mos.	1. Follows series of three simple related commands.[a] 2. Recognizes different sounds. 3. Demonstrates by appro-	1. Uses short sentences; "Daddy go bye-bye."[a] 2. Verbalizes toilet needs. 3. Uses pronouns but has syntax errors. Some inaccurate.

Continued

Table 1.—*Continued*

Age	Receptive language	Expressive language
	priate responses his understanding of action words. 4. Responds to phrases such as "show me." 5. Identifies familiar pictures on request.	4. Echoes the last two or three words of a rhyme. 5. Discards jargon. 6. Tells his full name. 7. Uses 25 percent of all consonants.
24 to 36 mos.	1. Carries out three verbal commands, given in one utterance.[a] 2. Understands "just one block" as a command. 3. Understands taking turns. 4. Follows commands using in, on, under prepositions.	1. Mother understands 90 percent of his communication attempts.[a] 2. Uses noun-verb combinations with correct verb tense. 3. Repeats three digits given intervals. 4. Refers to self by pronoun. 5. Names his siblings on request. 6. States sex and full name. 7. Relates his experiences. 8. Recites some rhymes or song. 9. Asks for personal help.

[a]Items that suggest referral even if other areas are adequate. If one or more of the footnoted items are not present, then a referral is suggested.

suspected, such as autistic-like behavior, emotional problems, hearing deficits, and mental retardation. Ultimately, school failure and learning disabilities may result. Early detection should prevent or ameliorate problems before the child enters school.

SUGGESTED READINGS

Bangs, T., and S. Garet. Early Childhood Education for the Handicapped Child, Birth–3 Scale. Office of Education Grant Project No. OE6-0-9-530-312-456 (618), U.S. Government Printing Office, Washington, D.C.

Bayley, N. 1969. Bayley Scales of Infant Development. The Psychological Corporation, New York.

Chomsky, N. 1972. Language and Mind. Harcourt Brace Jovanovich, Inc., New York.

Church, J. 1961. Language and the Discovery of Reality. Random House, New York.

Gesell, A. 1940. The First Five Years of Life. Harper and Row, New York.

Lenneberg, E. H. 1967. Biological Foundations of Language. John Wiley and Sons, Inc., New York.

Lewis, M. M. 1959. How Children Learn to Speak. Basic Books, New York.

Menyuk, P. 1971. The Acquisition and Development of Language. Prentice-Hall, Inc., Englewood Cliffs, N.J.

NUTRITION
AND THE CHILD

Philomena Lomena, M.S. *

The child's nutritional status is the sum total of the mother's nutritional status before pregnancy, her status during pregnancy, and the mother's ability to meet the child's needs at all stages of his development. Therefore, the nutritional life of the child really begins before birth, and the mother's diet during pregnancy is very much related to the status of the child in the area of nutrition. A poorly nourished mother gives her infant a poor start in life nutritionally.

NUTRITION DURING THE FIRST YEAR

Food is a vital factor during the first year of the child's life. The kind, amount, method of preparation, and manner of feeding are of primary importance for a healthy, happy baby. The growth rate is rapid during this first year; therefore, the nutrient requirements are high per unit of body weight. The growth rate is greatest during the first 6 months and then gradually begins to taper off towards the end of the year. Caloric and protein requirement per unit of body weight bears a direct relationship to the growth rate, being highest when the growth rate is greatest, as shown in Figure 1.

It is important to remember that a baby has very small body stores of needed nutrients, therefore he must rely very heavily on his daily food intake to supply him with his nutrient needs. The well nourished infant has all of these needs met and follows the normal growth pattern, gaining about 2 pounds per month during the first 3 months and then slowing down to about 1 pound per month (Figures 2 and 3). The baby almost doubles his birth weight in 6 months and triples it in a year. Growth in length follows a similar pattern. He increases about 20 percent in height in the first 3 months and shows a total increase of about 50 percent of the birth length in 1 year.

*Chief of Nutrition, John F. Kennedy Child Development Center, University of Colorado Medical Center, 4200 East 9th Avenue, Denver, Colorado 80220.

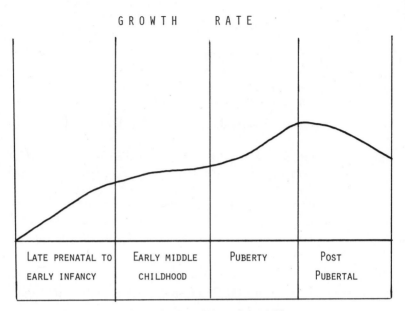

Figure 1. Growth rate of the child.

DIET

During this first year the infant relies heavily on milk for his needed nutrients. Like all other individuals, he needs protein for growth, involving body building and tissue repair; carbohydrates and fats for energy; vitamins and minerals to protect him against infections and disease entities; and adequate total calories for satiety and to support normal growth and development. Although milk supplies all of these nutrients except iron, it is inappropriate for the infant to rely on milk as the sole source of nutrients and calories. Milk is an adequate source of certain amino acids, the end products of protein; of some vitamins, such as vitamins A and D and riboflavin; and of some minerals, such as calcium and phosphorus. However, a variety of sources offers a better opportunity of supplying the infant with all of the nutrients from the major areas and allows for a more complete picture of good nutrition. By 4 to 6 weeks of age, other foods should begin to be introduced into the diet, such as cereal, with a progression to strained fruits, vegetables, and meat, so that by 5 to 6 months of age the child should be well on his way to a varied diet consisting of milk, fruit, vegetables, meat, and eggs. The consistency should gradually change from strained to "junior" to table food, and by 1

Figure 2. Six-month-old well nourished infant.

Figure 3. Six-month-old poorly nourished infant.

year of age the child should be well established on a variety of table foods.

Feeding Development

If table food is not introduced into the diet at a time that is consistent with the normal developmental profile (Table 1), the child is denied for an unnecessarily long period of time the opportunity to strengthen his facial muscles and oral peripheral areas involved in chewing. Feeding skill development may then be delayed and this may involve some delays in language development, since the same oral muscular development and oral peripheral areas involved in feeding are also involved in speech (U.S. Department of Agriculture, 1973).

Self-feeding skills should be encouraged as soon as signs of their emergence become evident. They should be fairly well established by the end of the first year so that the child drinks from a cup, finger feeds, and has attained beginning skills of spoon feeding. It should be remembered that each child is a unique individual and there will be variations in

Table 1.   Normal feeding development to 1 year[a]

0–4 weeks	Poor lip control and some difficulty sucking. Poor tongue control.
0–4 months	There is some tongue protrusion and food should be placed well back on the tongue.
5 months	Better lip control, and can approximate lips to cup. Can hold a spoon.
6–9 months	Coordination of tongue and lip during feeding, and less interference with tongue protrusion. Removes food from spoon with lips, not with teeth. Can drink from a cup held to the lips and help hold cup while drinking. Manipulates spoon and cup in play.
9–12 months	Finger feeding emerging with use of fine prehension. Picks up small pieces of food. Plays with feeding utensils (cup, spoon, dish) in a way that shows understanding of function.

Note: Feeding skills should be well developed by 2 years of age.

[a]Adapted from John F. Kennedy Child Development Center Feeding Development Profile.

the time at which infants accept and can tolerate solids and the time at which they acquire self-feeding skills. However, if there are no physical problems, they should operate within the normal range of development (see Tables 1 and 2).

Some Facts About Milk

Some important facts that should be borne in mind are the following. 1) Milk is a poor source of iron. Fetal iron stores, which are high at birth if maternal iron stores were good, begin to be gradually depleted. They are dangerously low by 6 months of age unless efforts are made to replenish the stores. 2) By 3 months of age, the child's diet should be a varied one and should include iron-rich foods such as cereals and meat. 3) Unless otherwise indicated, as in the case of obesity or fat intolerance, the child should be given whole milk since it is difficult to meet his total caloric needs on skim milk.

Use of Supplemental Vitamins

Until the child reaches the stage at which he is on a sufficiently varied diet to provide all of his needed nutrients, it is advisable to give supplemental vitamins. When the diet is sufficiently varied and if the child's appetite is good, supplemental vitamins are usually superfluous, since it is easy to exceed the recommended allowances of vitamins. A study of the vitamin A intake of 64 Denver children showed that after the first 3 months three-fourths of the children met the Recommended Dietary Allowance by diet alone. When supplemental vitamin A was given only 64 percent of the time, the median intake from all sources was 10,000 IU. The Recommended Dietary Allowance for children this age is 1,500 IU.

PRESCHOOL CHILD

Between the ages of two and six years growth rate decreases, as the growth chart (Figure 1) indicates. Weight gain is only about 4 to 5 pounds a year.

Table 2. Feeding development related to textures

0–1½	months	Milk
1½–2	months	Milk, cereal and fruit juices
3–6	months	Strained food
4–9	months	"Junior" food
9–12	months	Table food

Thus, the caloric needs and the needs of nutrients required for growth (e.g., vitamins, iron and protein) per kilogram of body weight decrease as shown in the Recommended Dietary Allowances (1973). Again, specific needs vary among different children, since their needs are influenced by such factors as rate of growth, activity, and status of health. In a broad frame of reference, however, it is suggested that between ages 1 and 3 years no less than 1,300 kilocalories are required, and between 4 and 6 years approximately 1,800 kilocalories (Recommended Dietary Allowances, 1973).

Diet

The diet of the preschool child, as for all other individuals, should be representative of the four basic food groups (Table 3) in amounts that would adequately supply the nutrient and caloric needs. Thus, the following is the daily recommendation.

Table 3. Food group and calorie equivalent[a]

Milk group:
   8 ounces of milk: whole milk   = 158 Kcal
                   low fat milk (20%) = 142 Kcal
                   nonfat milk (skim) = 86 Kcal
Meat group:
   10 ounces of meat,
         fish,
         or chicken or equivalents = 73 Kcal (approx.)
Fruit and vegetable group:
   1/2 cup vegetable, e.g., green peas, carrots, beets   = 36 Kcal
   1/2 cup fruit (canned in syrup)   = 80 Kcal
   Fresh fruit, e.g., apple, orange (medium size)   = 40 Kcal
   4 ounces of fruit juice, e.g., orange juice
   (fresh or frozen)   = 40 Kcal
Bread and cereal group:
   Equivalents of slice of bread (1 slice of bread = 68 Kcal)
                    1/2 cup cooked cereal
                    3/4 cup dry cereal (no sugar added)
                    1/2 cup rice
                    1/2 cup mashed potato
                    1 small boiled potato
                    1/2 cup spaghetti or macaroni
                    1/3 cup corn

---

[a]The sources of calorie levels are Composition of Foods Agriculture Handbook, No. 8, U. S. Department of Agriculture (1963), and American Dietetic Association Calories Exchange List.

Milk Group Three or more glasses are required. Cheese, ice cream, and other milk products can be used as part of the milk allowance.

	1½ ounces of cheese	8 ounces or 1 glass of milk
or	1¾ cube of American cheese	for calcium equivalent
or	1 cup cottage cheese	
and	1 ounce of cheese, 1¼ cube of American cheese, or 2 tablespoons of cottage cheese equals 8 ounces or 1 glass of milk for protein equivalents.	

Meat Group Two or more servings are needed.

Total requirement for the day:	Ages 1 to 3 years: two servings
	Ages 3 to 6 years: three servings
Protein equivalents are:	1 egg; 1 ounce of meat, fish or chicken; 1 ounce of cheese; 2 tablespoons of cottage cheese; ½ cup cooked dry beans; 2 tablespoons of peanut butter

Fruit and Vegetable Group One serving of a high vitamin C fruit, e.g., orange or grapefruit equal to 4 ounces of juice, one small orange, or ½ grapefruit plus one serving of a high vitamin A vegetable, viz., dark green leafy or yellow, one or more servings of other fruits and vegetables are needed.

Bread and Cereal Group Two or more servings are needed. These should be enriched or whole grain. Servings should be small to encourage children to eat and to give them a feeling of accomplishment after they have eaten.

Servings:

meat	½ or 1 ounce
potato (or substitute)	1 to 2 tablespoons
bread	½ to 1 slice
vegetable	2 tablespoons
fruit	2 tablespoons
milk	4 to 8 ounces

Food Habits of the Preschool Child

The preschool child is at that age where his will and ability to be independent are increasing. He begins to demonstrate this, often through food, by some negative behavior: "no," "I don't want to," "I don't like it." Those are examples of very typical responses one is likely to hear in dealing with a child in this age group. A tactful approach is needed with this kind of behavior. Do not force him. It is very important to remember that the table should not be turned into a battleground. This serves to increase behavior problems at meal time and also to entrench dislike for specific foods or for the whole feeding process. Meal time should be a happy time. Limits should be set to handle the negative behavior and there should be consistency in dealing with the child. The following facts are important when trying to encourage good food habits. 1) Food can be used as a reward to reinforce good food habits; for instance, desserts could be used to reward full participation in the main meal. 2) Food should never be used as "punishment." 3) Preschool children tend to be picky and to have erratic food habits. 4) They reject today what they will eat tomorrow. 5) The amount of food they eat may vary. 6) An item of food once rejected may be presented again with an item well liked. Color and flavor are useful tools in trying to create a pleasant atmosphere and encouraging a better appetite at meal time.

If the child's appetite is very picky and his intake is not enough to meet his nutrient needs, vitamin supplements are advisable.

SCHOOL AGE CHILD (6 TO 12 YEARS)

The school age child is very active and growth rate again begins to accelerate as the growth chart (Figure 1) indicates. His caloric and nutrient needs per kilogram of body weight begin to increase, and this is reflected in his increase in appetite. Usually the erratic eating behaviors of the preschool years have disappeared by this time and the child has developed very definite eating patterns. There are fewer dislikes and the child has a comparatively good appetite.

Food Habits

Food habits in the school age child are better formulated than in the preschool years. Care should be taken to see that these habits are consistent with an adequate dietary intake and acceptable forms of behavior at the table. This is important, because whether they are good or bad these are the habits that are likely to be carried through life. Empty calories from sweets and soda only serve to depress the appetite and to take the place of needed foods like fruits and vegetables and to promote dental caries. A country-wide survey shows that children's diets tend to be lacking in calcium, ascorbic acid, and vitamin A (Martin, 1972). Snacks have their place in a child's diet but should be selected from the milk, vegetable, and fruit groups.

Requirements

The diet should be representative of the four basic food groups: 1) the milk group, three or more servings; 2) the meat group, two or more servings with a total of 4 to 5 ounces; 3) the fruit and vegetable group, four or more servings including: one citrus or high vitamin C fruit and one high vitamin A vegetable; 4) the bread and cereal group, four or more servings.

The main difference between the diet of the preschool child and that of the school age child is the size of the servings. The preschool child requires smaller portions. What is lacking in quantity should certainly be made up for in quality.

Factors That Affect the Child's Food Intake

Some factors that affect food intake at all ages are: culture, economic status, food habits, age, and activity.

Culture Culture determines the kinds of food that are eaten and the kinds that may be taboo. It is important to first become familiar with the cultural food habits of the family to which the child belongs before beginning to assess the diet for any inadequacies. Necessary modifications to meet recommended standards may then be offered. Culture runs deep and is colored with emotional attachments. Therefore, cultural food habits cannot be changed, but with teaching and awareness could certainly be improved if this is necessary.

Economic Status This certainly affects the kind and amount of food a family can buy and, ultimately, the child's intake. For the family of limited income, education about budgeting and the kinds of food needed for a balanced diet is vital.

Food Habits Whether food habits are good or bad, they will affect what the child eats and does not eat, and are often related to the food habits of the entire family. Therefore, the child's food habits cannot be assessed in isolation, but must be considered in reference to family food habits.

Age and Activity The age of a child determines appetite and food needs, and activity determines the amount of calories needed. Under normal conditions, a child's appetite serves as the control mechanism in helping him to adjust to his food needs.

In conclusion, it is important to remember that nutrition during these early years, especially the first 6 years of life, plays a vital role in the development of the child physically, mentally, and emotionally.

LITERATURE CITED

Martin, E. N. 1963. Roberts' Nutrition Work with Children. University of Chicago Press, Chicago.
U.S. Department of Agriculture. 1963. Composition of Foods, Agriculture Handbook No. 8. U.S. Government Printing Office, Washington, D.C.

SUGGESTED READINGS

Fomon, S. J. 1973. Skim Milk in Infant Feeding. U.S. Department of Health, Education and Welfare, Maternal and Child Health Service, U.S. Government Printing Office, Washington, D.C.
Mueller, H.A. Facilitating feeding and prespeech. *In* P. Pearson and C.E. Williams, (eds.). Physical Therapy Services in the Developmentally Disabled. Charles C Thomas, Publisher, Springfield, Ill.
Office of Economic Opportunity. 1900. Nutrition—Better Eating for a Headstart. U.S. Government Printing Office, Washington, D.C.
Wilson, E.D., K. H. Fisher, and M. E. Fuqua. 1961. Principles of Nutrition. John Wiley & Sons, Inc., New York.

X
FAMILIES WITH CHILDREN AT RISK FOR SCHOOL PROBLEMS

William J. van Doorninck, Ph.D. *

Physical and genetic factors can have an obvious role in developmental delay, but readiness for school seems most frequently influenced by the child's home environment. An interesting milestone study by Werner and her colleagues (1971) of an entire population of children in Kauai, Hawaii gives an unusually full perspective on the histories of children with school problems.

The island of Kauai is generally lower in standard of living than a cross-section of the United States. Therefore, the results of Werner's study are mainly applicable to lower than average socioeconomic status (SES) groups. About one-third of Kauai children had substantial school problems (academic or behavioral) at age 10. The outcome of severe perinatal complications (PC) was impressive. Only 61 percent of newborns with severe PC survived until age 2. Among the survivors, about 58 percent had substantial school problems at age 10. School problems included one or more of the following: physical handicap, emotional problems, IQ below 85, and "D's" and "F's" in major subjects. Thus severe PC had a powerful influence on infant mortality and a persistent influence on later school adjustment among survivors; however, among the total group of 10-year-olds who experienced school failure, only 6 percent had histories of severe PC. In short, children who survive severe PC have a good chance of experiencing later handicap but represent a small fraction of the school problem group.

The families of the Kauai children were rated as to the degree of educational stimulation in the home. The rating reflected the education level of both parents, intellectual interests of the parents, the importance

*Psychologist and Assistant Professor, Department of Pediatrics, University of Colorado School of Medicine, 4200 East Ninth Avenue (C233), Denver, Colorado 80220.

151

of education for children shown by parents, opportunities provided for educational stimulation outside the home, and the amount of reading of books to the child in the preschool years. A sizeable percentage of families rated low in educational stimulation undoubtedly also came from the lowest social class with its higher incidence of family stresses. Thus, the rating probably reflected the often observed combination of high family stress, low resources, and low preparation of children for school. Families rated low in educational stimulation produced 75 percent of the school failures at age 10.

The correlation between SES and school achievement and other measures of competence in children has long been recognized. In fact, the Head Start program identified whole groups of children as "at risk" for later school problems because of family income. Werner's study suggested that, by rating families of varying SES levels according to evidence of educational stimulation, a higher proportion of school problems could be predicted.

HOME ASSESSMENT

The studies of Caldwell and her associates in Syracuse, New York and Little Rock, Arkansas have furthered our ability to measure "educational preparation" in homes. Caldwell and Richmond (1968) had searched extensively in the child development literature for family environment features most likely to influence development. From their review, a list of behavioral assessments was created. Some of these were scored "yes" or "no" by simply observing while in the family's home. For example, the home visitors would observe whether mother taught the child a new word during the home visit. Some items were scored after interviewing. For example, the home visitor might ask about mother's interests and note whether the family subscribed to a news magazine. A list of over 100 such items was revised and narrowed down according to how relevant the item was to the child's progress and how feasible the administration and scoring of the item were during a home visit.

Caldwell, Heider, and Kaplan (1966) described an early version of their Inventory of Home Stimulation, which was a longer version of the current HOME (Home Observation for Measurement of the Environment) scale. With the earlier version, Caldwell et al. (1966) were able to predict which lower class children would make the most gains in a preschool enrichment program. The children from homes scoring high on the home stimulation scale made higher gains. The expected relationship between the HOME scale and preschool development was confirmed by Elardo, Bradley, and Caldwell (1975). For example, 12-month-old infants in families scoring high on the HOME scale also scored high on their 12-, 24-, and 36-month mental tests. The categories of family assessment and illustrative items are given in Table 1.

This author reported a follow-up of elementary school children in Syracuse, New York (van Doorninck et al., 1975). The families of these children had been assessed with the earlier version of the HOME from 6 months of age. This study showed the possibilities for predicting school problems from family assessments. Forty-three percent of the children from lower class families had school problems. Only 7 percent of the higher social class had children with school problems. These figures compare favorably with the Kauai study in which 55 percent of the lowest class and 19 percent of the highest social class of children suffered school problems. Thus, in both Kauai and Syracuse, one could simply have picked families as "high risk" because of the SES and thereby net most of the future school problems. However, this selection procedure includes a large number of low SES children who do well in school. In the Syracuse sample, 56 percent of the low SES children had no reported school problems. These low SES, high achievement families would have been needlessly identified and "assisted" with supplemental programs.

The overinclusion of Syracuse children in the high risk group was corrected significantly (by hindsight) by using the home stimulation assessment to classify children at risk. Table 2 shows the "hits" as well as the "misses" when predicting school status from 12-month home assessments.

Table 1. Categories of HOME assessments and illustrative items

---

I. Emotional and verbal responsivity of the mother
   Example: Mother responds to child's vocalizations with a vocal or verbal response.
II. Avoidance of restriction and punishment
   Example: Mother does not shout at child during visit.
III. Organization of physical and temporal environment
   Example: Child has a special place in which to keep his toys and "treasures."
IV. Provision of appropriate play materials
   Example: Mother provides learning equipment to age—mobile, table and chairs, highchair, playpen.
V. Maternal involvement with child
   Example: Mother structures child's play periods.
VI. Opportunities for variety in daily stimulation
   Example: Mother reads stories to child at least three times weekly.

Table 2. Predictive accuracy of family assessments

Family assessment total score	School status		
	Problems	Normal	Totals
Low	16	8	24
High	10	42	52
Totals	26	50	76

Notice that home assessment total scores were divided into "low" and "high" in Table 2. The most accurate division of total scores for this particular group of children was used. If a different group was assessed, the accuracy level would drop some, if the division point or "cut-off" score was not also changed.

Among the low home assessment children, 16 of 24 or 67 percent developed school problems. Among the high home assessment children, 42 of 52 or 81 percent had no school problems. This accuracy level is high, considering the variety of possible influences on a child between his 12th month and elementary school age. The accuracy level compares favorably to that reported for prediction of school problems from assessments of the child's preschool developmental skills (see Camp et al., 1974).

The significance of family assessments such as the HOME seems high; however, more long term studies are needed to confirm the degree of significance and establish the best cut-off score. Families scoring below this score might be informed of the likelihood (not the certainty) of future school problems for their child and that supplemental experiences might help. Families scoring above this cut-off should not be imposed upon with predictions of later school problems. Available evidence is scant, but Ramey et al. (1975) and van Doorninck et al. (1975) suggest that a HOME total score of 30 or less is indicative of "at risk" status. Obtaining reliable and valid scores depends on the interviewers' skills. The following are suggested guidelines for mastery. 1) Master the HOME items and interviewing format according to Caldwell's manual.[1] 2) For each interview, have an additional observer score as well. Over 10 consecutive practice interviews, 90 percent or more of the items (40 or more of the 45) are scored the same when one person interviews and scores and an observer scores the

---

[1] Information, forms and manual for the HOME Scale can be obtained from Bettye M. Caldwell, Ph.D., Center for Early Development and Education, 814 Sherman Street, Little Rock, Arkansas 72202.

same interview. 3) By developing a relaxed conversation style, in which the interviewer's interest in the well being of the parents is clearly conveyed, the interviewer avoids irritating or intimidating parents with questions in the HOME Scale areas.

Remember that the specific HOME items may be symptomatic of either normal or at risk status. They are not diagnostic or causal. For example, low achieving families, as a group, may not have live houseplants. The absence of a houseplant does not cause problems for the child, but the absence may be symptomatic of depression and its accompanying low energy for caring for and involving oneself in objects and outside activities. The absence may be symptomatic of parental disorganization with its accompanying inability to arrange over an extended period the proper nutrients for a live plant. Dysorganization may be itself symptomatic of low competence, marital stress, the loss of a loved person, severe stress, a lack of interest. The point to be made is that we do not know from the HOME scale the reasons for low scores. We should not attempt to supply them, because our explanations are apt to be too shallow. If taken seriously, our explanations can lead us and the family into mistaken conclusions and actions. Although using this initial assessment, one accepts the unexplained relationship between HOME total scores and the developmental progress of children. The need to explain will lead to diagnostic activities such as a longer term relationship with the family, a careful history, and educated guesswork.

SUPPLEMENTAL EXPERIENCES

HOME assessments in applied settings will probably be used to identify families whose members need supplemental services designed to offset later delays in the development of their children.

In the applied setting, it would be unethical to assess families and then have nothing to offer those for whom some unfortunate outcome is predicted. Preschools and day care centers for children of 3 years and more are now generally available. However, the evaluations of the large numbers of demonstration projects in early cognitive stimulation have left us with the impression that the initiation of intervention should begin during the 15- to 36-month period for maximum effect on the child (see Starr, 1971). This age period happens to coincide with the most rapid development in language skills. Traditionally, among child development specialists, proficiency with language has been the most highly prized area of the child's performance on tests in preschools and elementary schools. Future research will discover the means by which infants acquire the nonlanguage cognitive tools which enhance later development. The recent book by Burton White (1975) probably contains the most important current knowledge of the environmental influences on cognitive development before age 3. A book like this will stimulate a more sophisticated technology of practical interventions. In the meantime, interventions currently available are known to be beneficial. Examples will be given from omnibus, parent-oriented, and child-oriented programs.

Omnibus programs provide comprehensive services to parents and children. The Syracuse University Children's Center, begun in 1964, is one of the oldest of its kind (see Caldwell and Richmond, 1964; 1968). Parent education groups, some sick child care, social services to parents, involvement of parents in the educational activities with children, a 6- to 9-hour program day, 5 days a week for children from 6 months of age and older, and nutritional education were provided. Babies, toddlers, and parents benefited from this program. The degree of benefit varied with the quality of the family environment as assessed by earlier versions of the HOME scale. Home Start, a federal effort by the Office of Child Development and the Department of Health, Education and Welfare, qualifies as an omnibus program. Home Start has been a demonstration project for local Head Start programs. This home-based program includes early childhood education, health, social services and parent involvement as its major components. The June 1974 Guide for Planning and Operating Home-Based Child Development Programs[2] provides the details for implementing such programs, when agency support is possible.

A child-centered program, the Infant Education Research Project (Schaefer, 1969), was also conducted in the home. The children were very poor black children, who entered the program at 14 months of age and continued until age 3. An informal but carefully planned curriculum stressing cognitive and language skills was used. This program was successful insofar as the program children at three years of age had average intelligence test scores. The same type of children, without this program, dropped to IQ scores in the high 80's by age 3. However, an unpublished follow-up of the program children showed a decline in their IQ scores 1 year after the program termination. Schaefer, through personal communication, shared his conviction that early child development programs must involve parents. Without parent involvement, the disadvantaged child would need outside tutoring over an extended period from toddlerhood through elementary school.

---

[2] This guide can be obtained from Office of Child Development, Department of Health, Education and Welfare, Home Start, P.O. Box 1182, Washington, D.C. 20013.

A good example of a parent-centered program is the Mother-Child Home Program (Levenstein, 1970; Levenstein et al., 1973). The curriculum materials were developed for 24- to 48-month-old children. The home visitor takes on the function of a "Toy Demonstrator." In this capacity, she visits the home for ½-hour sessions, two per week, over a 2-year period, excluding school holidays and vacations. During each visit a new toy or book is introduced and the visitor demonstrates for the mother its use with the child. The play materials and techniques are carefully designed to elicit language skills in the child. Family and personal problems of the mother are likely to arise, but the toy demonstrator refers the mother to supportive services. In this manner, the home session maintains the focus on how to use the toys and books with the child. No direct teaching of the mother is involved. Rather, through observation, and by slowly trying out the play techniques with her child, the mother models after the toy demonstrator and becomes the principal facilitator of play with her child between visits and after program termination.

The Mother-Child Home Program[3] has been successful with mothers, some of whom have subsequently become toy demonstrators for others. The children made impressive gains in intelligence test scores and maintained those gains into the primary grades.

A number of early childhood programs focused on parenting skills have appeared. They are reviewed and evaluated by Lazar and Chapman (1972) in *The Present Status and Future Research Needs of Programs to Develop Parenting Skills.*[4]

The overall impression from reviews of early childhood programs is that parent involvement is highly desirable, that home visits are more economical in terms of cost and time well spent, that parenting skills need to be altered for greater persistence of the desired effects. Gains in child skills are possible at any age from 6 months to school age, but the 15- to 36-month period is potentially the period allowing greatest impact of supplemental stimulation. The exact curriculum used is not important as long as language skills and vocabulary are stressed and the activities with parent and child are well planned and enjoyable. The primary goal for infants less than 15 months would be to stimulate mother's observation and enjoyment of the baby through demonstrated exercises and games. An excellent program for infants is Gordon's (1970) Baby Learning through Baby Play.

---

[3] The manual for this relatively inexpensive program can be obtained from the Verbal Interaction Project/Mother-Child Home Program, 5 Broadway, Freeport, Long Island, New York 11520.

[4] This report can be obtained from Social Research Group, George Washington University, Washington, D.C.

Readers interested in developing a home visit program for purposes of enhancing the developmental progress of young children should acquaint themselves with the formal programs presented here. The necessary details are presented in the manuals. When it is not feasible to implement or utilize existing programs, informal constructions are still possible. A good example is the Krajicek et al. (1973) *Stimulation Activities Guide for Children from Birth to 5 Years*. This guide was based upon more elaborate resources, as can be found in *Parent Resource Library Catalogue*.[5] The "Parent Catalogue" is generally useful for a large variety of problems with all ages of children. One section is devoted to developing learning at home.

LITERATURE CITED

Caldwell, B. M., J. Heider, and B. Kaplan. 1966. The inventory of home stimulation. Paper presented at the meeting of the American Psychological Association, September 1966.

Caldwell, B. M., and J. B. Richmond. 1964. Programmed day care for the very young child—A preliminary report. J. Marriage Fam. 26: 481—488.

Caldwell, B. M., and J. B. Richmond. 1968. The Children's Center in Syracuse, New York. *In* L. Dittman (ed.), Early Child Care: The New Perspectives, pp. 326—358. Atherton Press, New York.

Camp, B. W., W. J. van Doorninck, W. K. Frankenburg, and J. M. Lampe. 1974. Follow-up of preschool developmental screening. Paper presented at the Western Society for Pediatric Research meetings in Carmel, California, February 1974.

Elardo, R., R. Bradley, and B. M. Caldwell. 1975. The relation of infant's home environments to mental test performances—6—36 months: A longitudinal analysis. Child Devel. 46: 71—76.

Gordon, I. 1970. Baby Learning through Baby Play. St. Martin's Press, New York.

Krajicek, M. J., C. Turner, P. Barnes, and W. Borthick. 1973. Stimulation Activities Guide for Children from Birth to 5 Years. John F. Kennedy Child Development Center, University of Colorado Medical Center, Denver, Colorado.

Lazar, J. B., and J. E. Chapman. 1972. A review of the present status and future research needs of programs to develop parenting skills. Prepared for the Interagency Panal on Early Childhood Research and Development (OCD Grant No. OCD CB 107).

Levenstein, P. 1970. Cognitive growth in preschoolers through verbal interaction with mothers. Amer. J. Orthopsych. 40: 426—432.

Levenstein, P., A. Kochman, and H. A. Roch. 1973. From laboratory to real world: Service delivery of the Mother-Child Home Program. Amer. J. Orthopsych. 43: 72—78.

---

[5] This catalogue can be obtained from the Exceptional Child Center, Utah State University, Logan, Utah 84322.

Ramey, C. T., P. Mills, F. A. Campbell, and C. O'Brien. 1975. Infants' home environments: A comparison of high-risk families and families from the general population. Amer. J. Ment. Defic. 80: 40–42.

Schaefer, E. S. 1969. A home turoring program. Children 16: 59–61.

Starr, R. H., Jr. 1971. Cognitive development in infancy: Assessment, acceleration and actualization. Merrill-Palmer Quart. 17: 153–186.

van Doorninck, W. J., B. M. Caldwell, C. Wright, and W. K. Frankenburg. 1975. The relationship between the 12-month Inventory of Home Stimulation and school competence. Paper presented at the meeting of the Society for Research in Child Development, Denver, Colorado, April 1975.

Werner, E.E., J. M. Bierman, and F. E. French. 1971. The Children of Kauai. University of Hawaii Press, Honolulu.

White, B. L. 1975. The First Three Years of Life. Prentice-Hall, Englewood Cliffs, N.J.

XI
BEHAVIOR MODIFICATION: USE WITH CHILDREN

Nancy Matthews Weaver, B.S., M.S. *
Marilyn J. Krajicek, R.N., M.S. †

Behavior modification is a useful tool for nurses and other health care professionals to have in working with a child with problems, in helping parents relate more effectively to their children, or in assisting a teacher to help a child in her class. Parents and teachers have questions about the role they play when relating to their children and want to help them grow in the most healthy way, both physically and mentally. They need to know more about the principles of behavior modification, and professionals can guide them in learning about this effective way of relating to children.

This chapter explores useful behavior modification techniques, and how a nurse can use them in his or her own relationship with children, as well as in helping parents and teachers relate to their children in a positive and consistent way. Terms used in behavior modification are defined and observation and data collecting methods are explained.

DEFINITIONS OF TERMS USED IN BEHAVIOR MODIFICATION

Reinforcement is a consequence following a behavior which will increase that behavior.

> *Example:* A child will pick up his toys, if each time he does his mother lets him know how much she appreciates his efforts.

Punishment is a consequence following a behavior which will decrease that behavior.

> *Example:* If a child is told to sit in a chair each time he hits his sister, the child will stop hitting his sister.

---

*Educational Consultant, Denver, Colorado.

†Chief Nurse, John F. Kennedy Child Development Center; Instructor, Department of Pediatrics, School of Medicine; Assistant Clinical Professor, School of Nursing, University of Colorado Medical Center, 4200 E. 9th Avenue, Denver, Colorado 80220.

Extinction is not responding to a behavior in order to decrease that behavior.

Example: A child engaging in temper tantrums who is not given attention by his mother (ignored), will stop tantruming.

Shaping is reinforcing closer and closer approximations to the desired behavior.

Example: In working with a mother around toilet training her two-year-old child, the procedure must be broken down step by step and each step rewarded. Suggested sequence:

1. The child should be taken to the bathroom approximately every 2 hours. Mother should reinforce the child for going with her to the bathroom and sitting on the potty.
2. Next, mother should continue taking the child every 2 hours, but reinforce the child only when he uses the toilet.
3. When mother takes the child to the bathroom, she should reinforce him only when he is dry and then uses the toilet.
4. When child indicates by gesturing or vocalization a need to go to the bathroom, mother should take the child and then reinforce him for indicating his need. Continue taking him on a regular schedule and reinforcing him for being dry and going in the toilet.
5. Mother should reinforce the child for his assistance in pulling his pants down, for going in the toilet, and for his assistance in pulling his pants up.
6. Mother should reinforce the child for pulling his pants down, for going in the toilet, and for pulling his pants up by himself.
7. Mother should reinforce the child for completing the entire toileting process by himself.

Each of the above steps could take several weeks, depending on the child's readiness, so be patient. As the child moves from step to step, drop out the reinforcer for the previous step.

Consistency is following through with a selected approach.

Example: A mother is trying to get her child to drink a 4-ounce glass of milk at meals. She reinforces him *each time* he finishes a glass.

Example: Each time a child gets out of bed after he has been put to bed, the parent needs to immediately return him to bed.

Observation is watching behavior for a specific period of time in order to determine the frequency of the behavior's occurrence.

Example: A child has frequent temper tantrums in preschool; the teacher records the number of times she observes the child have a temper tantrum.

Recording is the systematic record keeping of the number of times a behavior occurs (Figure 1).

Consequence is the event that follows the occurrence of a behavior.

> *Example:* A child finishes his dinner and as a reward (consequence) receives a dessert.

Baseline is the frequency of occurrence of a behavior prior to intervention.

> *Example:* An observer records the frequency of whining behavior before attempts are made to change that behavior.

Manipulation is the intervention technique introduced in order to change a behavior.

> *Example:* A child throws his toys. In order to decrease the throwing behavior, the child is placed in a chair each time he throws his toys.

OBSERVATION

Accurate observations must occur before any procedures are undertaken to modify a behavior. One must communicate to the parent or teacher that the observation is being done to select an appropriate intervention technique. It is necessary to *know*, through observation, what behaviors the subject is emitting rather than assuming or accepting that a behavior

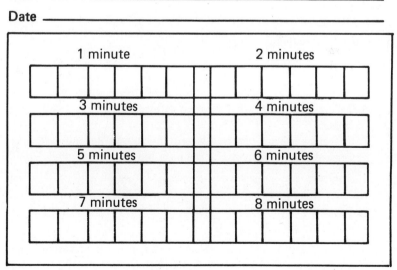

Child's name _____

Date _____

Figure 1. Sample of a chart for systematic record keeping of times a behavior occurs.

occurs on hearsay. When observing, it is important to remain silent and not interact with the child or any other people in the environment. An observation is done in two steps. The first step is the running record. The second is the objective observation.

Running Record

This method is used so that one will get an idea of what behaviors are occurring and what behaviors need to be modified. This observation is done by observing the subject for 30 minutes, two different times in his or her natural environment (home, school, etc.), and writing down as much as possible of what is seen. One needs to include those behaviors that seem inappropriate and the events that occur before (stimulus) and after those behaviors (consequences). It is important to observe the parent or teacher's behavior in interacting with the child. Also, from this observation, a particular behavior can be identified to use in making a more objective observation.

Example:

NAME: Janet Brown (let "S" stand for subject)
DATE: 6/4/73
TIME: 10:04 A.M.
PLACE: Home.

S is going to get a cookie from the cookie jar—pulls chair over—climbs up on counter—mother says, "no, no"—mother gets S down—S cries and throws herself on floor—mother gives cookie—etc.,—etc.

Objective Observation

An objective observation is made to accurately count the number of times a certain behavior occurs. In this observation the observer need not use his or her subjective judgment, but should define what he or she is observing and record only what has been defined.

Example:

If the behavior being observed is tantruming or getting out of bed, the observer should define those behaviors as follows:

1. Tantrum—the subject cries, screams, throws himself on the floor and holds his breath.
2. Getting out of bed—Any point at which no part of the body touches the bed.

After defining what behavior is being observed, prepare a recording sheet on which to record the behaviors. Figure 2 is an example of a recording sheet. In this figure, each square represents 10 seconds. Each group of six

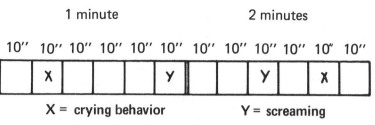

1 minute   2 minutes

10" 10" 10" 10" 10" 10" 10" 10" 10" 10" 10" 10"

X = crying behavior   Y = screaming

Figure 2. Recording sheet. See text for explanation.

squares represents a minute. Designate a symbol to represent the behavior, such as "X." Start at the first square, moving the pencil from square to square as each 10-second interval passes (Figure 3). You will need to have a watch with a second hand or a stop watch. Place a symbol in the 10-second square in which the behavior occurs each time it occurs. After 30 minutes of observation, count the number of times the behavior occurred during the observation. Make a graph and record the number of times the behavior occurred on the graph (Figure 4). You will need to do three of these observations.

With the baseline data (see definition) begin to work with a teacher or a parent around changing a behavior. This technique of observing and recording will also help you to train yourself to be a better observer.

Parent or Teacher Observation

Once one knows what behaviors need to be modified, it is important to talk to the parent or teacher about what behaviors they see as needing to be changed. Together, agree on *one* behavior to change. *Caution:* It is a great temptation to want to change many behaviors at one time. Do not give into this temptation! Choose only *one!* The parents or teacher needs to be aware of how often the inappropriate behavior occurs. Often it is difficult for parents or teachers to be consistent when charting or responding to a child's behavior, but it is necessary for them to learn consistency in order

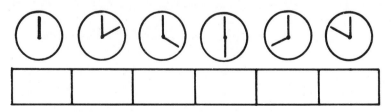

Figure 3. Recording sheet showing 10-second intervals.

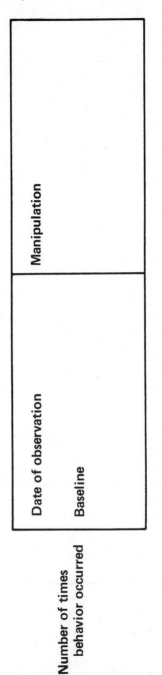

Figure 4. Graph of number of times behavior has occurred.

for behavior change to occur. Make a chart for the parent or teacher. The chart should be placed in an area of easy accessibility. A good idea is to tape it to the wall. Have them mark each time the behavior occurs.

An example of a chart which can be used by a parent or a teacher is shown in Figure 5. The chart should be kept for at least 4 days. At the end of the 4 days, review the chart with the parents or teacher and determine the behavior pattern and an intervention technique. Refer to definitions and see Intervention Suggestions. Parents or teachers should continue to chart the behavior after the intervention is begun so they will see it decrease. *Warning:* Oftentimes after manipulation occurs there is a testing period during which time the behavior occurrence will increase. This is normal and it is important to help the parent or teacher get through this time and see a change.

Follow-up Observation

After the manipulation has been in progress for 2 weeks, do two more objective observations and put the data on the original graph (Figure 4) on the manipulation side. After the third week of manipulation, do a third observation and chart the results (Figure 6). If the behavior is not changing, you will need to try another manipulation.

INTERVENTION SUGGESTIONS

Oftentimes the same techniques can be applied to the same problem behaviors in different children. Here are some suggestions for intervention.

1. The child may have temper tantrums when he does not get what he wants or when he must do something he doesn't want to do.

Inappropriate behavior

Baseline		Intervention	
Mon.	Oct. 1 ⦸⦸ ⦸⦸ /	Fri.	Oct. 5 ⦸⦸ ⦸⦸ ⦸⦸
Tues.	Oct. 2 ⦸⦸ ⦸⦸	Sat.	Oct. 6 ⦸⦸ /
Wed.	Oct. 3 ⦸⦸ ⦸⦸	Sun.	Oct. 7 ⦸⦸
Thurs.	Oct. 4 ⦸⦸ ⦸⦸		

Figure 5. Chart for parent or teacher.

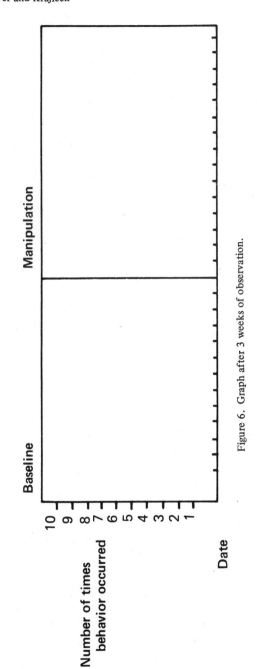

Figure 6. Graph after 3 weeks of observation.

When a child is having a tantrum, it is frequently difficult for an adult to withhold attention. A suggested intervention is ignoring the child for as long as the tantrum is in progress, and reinforcing the child when the tantruming behavior has stopped. A good way to reinforce the child is to help him get involved in another activity following the episode.

2. Other discipline problems which parents often must handle include: engaging in over-aggressive behavior toward siblings, getting into refrigerator, throwing toys and other items, refusing to perform a task when told to do so.

When trying to get rid of the above behaviors, a parent or teacher must be consistent with whatever form of management is used. Oftentimes, when consistent limit setting is used, the behavior gets worse before it gets better. Parents need help to get through this critical time of maintaining limit setting. It has been demonstrated that putting a child in the same chair in the same place and requiring him to sit there for 3 minutes or less is an effective means of decreasing inappropriate behavior. The child may try several times to get out of the chair but must be returned to the chair and told firmly to sit there.

3. The parent may experience a problem of the child not remaining at the table during a meal. Sitting at the table throughout the meal is a reasonable expectation for a normal 4-year-old child.

a. The parent should communicate his expectations to the child— "Johnny, you need to stay at the table during dinner."
b. If the child gets down from the table, the parent should place the child back at the table and give one warning—"Johnny, if you get down from the table again, you will not get any more to eat."
c. If the child will not stay at the table, the parent should ignore the child when he is away from the table and not give him any solid food until the next scheduled eating time.

4. The child may have a "picky" appetite. He may refuse to eat what the parent has prepared for a meal and only eat selected foods. This behavior may have become a habit which has existed for a long period of time. Often the parent has to prepare a separate meal for this child. In order to change this behavior, consider the following:

a. Introduce 2 teaspoonsful of a food which the child has previously refused.
b. Tell the child that he will get dessert when he cleans his plate. (Remember to give him small portions of all foods.)
c. Reinforce the child for eating new food and cleaning his plate. Do not get discouraged if child will not clean his plate. Continue to

introduce new foods by using the above method. It is important for the adult to remain calm and not to demonstrate disappointment if the child does not eat the new food. Be consistent in your approach. Do not give the child dessert if he does not clean his plate.

5. The child may refuse to stay in bed.

a. Parents should put a night light in the child's room if the child is afraid of the dark.
b. Parents should establish a routine to perform each night which may consist of bathing time, putting pajamas on, getting a drink, telling family members "goodnight," going to the bathroom, and/or reading a story to the child.
c. After this routine, the child needs to know it is time to go to sleep and remain in his bed.
d. Parents should ignore a child's request, whining, or crying if they are sure nothing is wrong. It is often difficult to ignore this behavior.
e. If the child gets out of bed and makes a request, the parent should not fulfill his request, but put him back in bed immediately, and tell him firmly, "You must stay in bed." Getting up and being put back to bed may occur several times for several nights until the child stays in bed. The parent needs to be consistent in his response to the child. Be patient in handling this behavior.

6. Toilet training—Refer to definition of *shaping*.

FADING OUT THE MANIPULATION

When and how does the parent or teacher drop out the manipulation and still maintain the desired behavior? This is a difficult question. The answer depends upon the individual child and situation. Once the desired behavior is achieved, such as toilet training, remaining at the table, or staying in bed, the manipulation procedure is no longer necessary. However, if the behavior appears again, reintroduce the manipulation procedure.

MAINTAINING DESIRED BEHAVIOR

In order to maintain any desired behavior such as picking up toys and putting them away, self-dressing, carrying out requests of others, or self-entertaining when mother is busy, it is important to consistently reinforce these behaviors. Oftentimes, attention is given to the child only when he is misbehaving. This pattern needs to be reversed and emphasis given to positive behavior.

Example: Usually when a child is quietly looking at a book, he is ignored by the adult. However, when he begins to tear the pages, he is given attention by being reprimanded. Although this may be considered punishment, if it is the only attention the child gets he will learn to misbehave in order to get attention.

CONCLUSION

Behavior modification, if appropriately used, will change undesirable behaviors and increase desirable ones. If the behaviors identified as needing to be changed appear to be complex, it is advisable to consult with a person who has expertise in the concepts of behavior modification. The key to a successful program for changing behavior is consistency.

The following two studies describe common behavior problems that can be changed by parents, teachers, and others interacting with children.

STUDY 1

AUTHORS: Marydel Couch and Hector Ayala
TITLE: Reducing Pouting Behavior Through Social Reinforcement of Non-Pouting.
SOURCE: Education 118, University of Kansas.

POPULATION AND SETTING: Crista was a bright, active first-grade girl. An only child, she was described as well-behaved and well-adjusted. The parents were concerned, however, because she frequently pouted. The parents had tried scolding, isolation, ignoring, and reasoning in attempting to deal with the problem but had had little success in decreasing its rate.

BEHAVIOR MEASURED: Crista's mother recorded a pouting event whenever Crista showed displeasure by making facial grimaces and isolating herself. Recording sessions were made from 7:30 to 8:30 P.M. each evening just prior to Crista's bedtime. Reliability checks were made by the father, who acted as a second independent observer, 13 times during the course of the experiment. In all cases the records were in complete agreement.

EXPERIMENTAL PROCEDURES AND RESULTS: *Baseline*$_1$: A 13-day baseline record of the operant level of pouting yielded a mean rate of 3.07 per hour (see Figure 7). *Praise for Not Pouting*$_1$: On the 14th day, Crista's parents began praising her throughout the day contingent on nonpouting. At times their praise

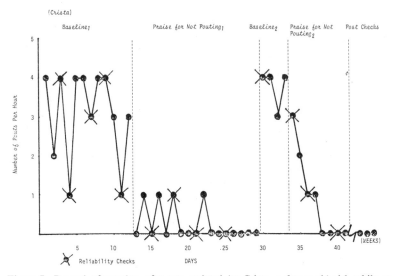

Figure 7. Record of number of pouts emitted by Crista, a 6-year-old girl, while at home, during a daily 1-hour observation session. Reproduced from Hall (1971c), p. 32, by permission of H & H Enterprises, Lawrence, Kansas.

and attention was accompanied by sweets and other rewarding consequences such as choosing where the family would have Sunday dinner. In this phase, pouting immediately decreased in rate to a mean rate of 0.24 per hour with none in the last four sessions. The four that were recorded occurred when Crista was told to get ready for bed. *Baseline₂*: On the 31st day Crista was told she had been doing a fine job and she was such a happy girl her parents would no longer need to notice every time she had a nice smiling face. The parents returned to ignoring or scolding Crista when she pouted. Pouting immediately returned. The mean level for this phase was 3.75 pouts per hour. *Praise for Not Pouting₂*: When the parents began praising Crista once more for not pouting the number of pouts quickly decreased to zero. *Post Checks:* Post checks were made at 1-week intervals over the next 3 weeks. Even though the parents made reinforcement more intermittent over this period there was no return of pouting behavior.

DISCUSSION: Systematic praise and attention to nonpouting behavior were effective in modifying pouting behavior of a 6-year-old girl. The parents reported that before the study they had experienced feelings of distress, frustration, and hopelessness at their inability to cope with pouting. After modification they expressed joy in their new-found relationship with their daughter.

STUDY 2

AUTHORS: Donald R. Lamb, Jasper Harris, and Rodney Copeland
TITLE: A Reinforcement Program for Returning an Eight-Year-Old Girl to Her Own Bed.
SOURCE: Education 118, University of Kansas.

POPULATION AND SETTING: The subject of this study was an 8-year-old girl from an upper middle class socioeconomic home. She had no history of chronic illness and was in excellent health. When little she had been allowed to come to her parents' bed to sleep at night when frightened or ill. After a time, however, she was leaving her bed to sleep with her parents even when not frightened or ill. As she got older, this became irritating to her parents.

BEHAVIOR MEASURED: The parents devised a chart. On it they marked whether or not she left her bed and came to her parents' bed. On several occasions the parents independently recorded the behavior as did the girl during the first experimental phase. There was always 100 percent agreement on their records.

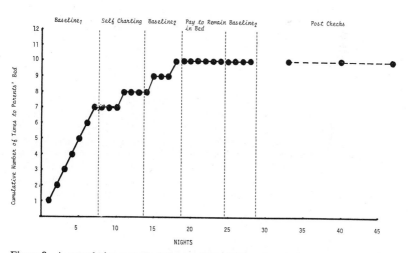

Figure 8. A cumulative record of the number of times that an 8-year-old girl left her bed to come to her parents' bed to sleep. Reproduced from Hall (1971c) p. 34, by permission of H & H Enterprises, Lawrence, Kansas.

EXPERIMENTAL PROCEDURES AND RESULTS: *Baseline*₁ : During a
7-night baseline phase, their daughter came to the parents'
bed every night (100 percent of the time). A cumulative
record of the number of times she came to her parents' bed is
shown in Figure 8. *Self-Charting*: Beginning on the eighth
night the parents showed their daughter the chart and told
her she could mark each morning whether or not she had
remained in her own bed all night. In this phase she came to
her parents' bed only once or 17 percent of the time. *Baseline*₂: Over the next 5 days the parents took back the chart
and recorded without their daughter's knowledge. She came
to their bed twice or 40 percent of the time. *Pay for Remaining in Bed*: Beginning on the 19th day of the experiment the
parents told their daughter that for every night she remained
in her own bed they would give her a nickel. They also
praised her when she remained in her bed every night. *Baseline*₃: After 6 days the parents removed the nickel con-
tingency and told their daughter she was doing very well and
no longer needed the help of receiving a nickel each morning.
The parents continued to mark the chart. Under these conditions she continued to remain in her bed each night. *Post
Check*: Over the next 3 weeks the parents made a formal post
check 1 night each week. These checks corroborated their
casual observation that their daughter had remained in her
bed all night every night.

DISCUSSION: This study is of interest because it deals with a behavior
which is a problem in many families. It is not experimentally
rigorous. The second baseline phase could have been extended
and the first experimental phase reinstituted. Understandably,
however, the parents sought a more powerful consequence in
order to eliminate the problem behavior entirely. Even
though they fully expected their daughter to come to their
bed when they instituted *Baseline*₃ she did not do so. Although causality was not shown, it can be assumed that her
parents' praise and the knowledge that she was able to stay in
her own bed were reinforcing enough to maintain her behavior
once it was established. It is, of course, the goal of most
modification studies to maintain behaviors with naturally
occurring reinforcers. (Notice that a cumulative record rather
than a conventional graph was used to record the number of
times the daughter went to her parents' bed.)

SUGGESTED READINGS

Barnard, K. 1968. Teaching the retarded child is a family affair. Amer. J.
Nurs. 68 (2).
Becker, W. 1971. Parents Are Teachers. Research Press, Champaign, Ill.

Bijou, S. W., and D. M. Baer. 1961. Child Development. Vol. 1. Appleton-Century-Crofts, New York.

Bijou, W., and D. M. Baer. 1967. Child Development: Readings in Experimental Analysis. Appleton-Century-Crofts, New York.

Cain, E. 1974. How Parents Can Shape or Change Their Children's Behavior. Colorado Department of Health, Denver. Colo.

Hall, V. R. 1971a. Behavior Modification: The Measurement of Behavior, #1, H & H Enterprises, Lawrence, Kan.

Hall, V. R. 1971b. Behavior Modification: Basic Principles, #2. H & H Enterprises, Lawrence, Kan.

Hall, V. R. 1971c. Behavior Modification: Application in School and Home, #3. H & H Enterprises, Lawrence, Kan.

Panyan, M. 1972. Behavior Modifications: New Ways to Teach New Skills, #4. H & H Enterprises, Lawrence, Kan.

Patterson, G. 1971. Families. Research Press, Champaign, Ill.

Patterson, G., and M. E. Gullion. 1968. Living with Children. Research Press, Champaign, Ill.

Ullman, L. P., and L. Krasner (eds.). 1965. Case Studies in Behavior Modification. Holt, Rinehart and Winston, New York.

Whitney, L. R., and K. E. Barnard. 1966. Implications of operant learning theory for nursing care of the retarded child. Ment. Retard. 4: 26–29.

XII
ROLE OF THE PUBLIC HEALTH NURSE IN CASES OF CHILD ABUSE

Brian G. Fraser, J.D. *

Alan, a 2-month-old boy, was admitted to the hospital for a failure to thrive, with malnutrition and dehydration. He (at 2 months) weighed less than ½ pound over his birth weight. While in the hospital he gained over a pound in 9 days. The welfare department filed a dependency petition, the juvenile court awarded temporary custody to the department, and the baby was placed in foster care. A rehearing of the case was planned after a 3-month interval, during which time the mother received general counseling, belonged to a young mothers' group, and had support from the welfare department. In the last 2 months of counseling, a great deal of progress was made and at the next court hearing the child was ordered to be returned to home, with the stipulation that there must be continuing contact with the welfare worker and a medical followup every 3 weeks. The mother and the child are now thriving.

A neighbor of 4-year-old David became concerned when she noticed a large number of bruises on the little boy. She soon learned that the stepmother beat the child and on occasion left him alone for long periods of time. She contacted various authorities for instructions on how best to help the child and was advised to try to become friendly and helpful to the mother, but if the child was left alone again to call the police. The next day the child *was* left alone, she called the police, who arrived 2 hours later (5 minutes after the mother had returned home). The neighbors, a preschool teacher, and a psychologist contacted the welfare department regarding the child's home environment. The stepmother was encouraged to go to the welfare department and ask for help. She told welfare that frankly she could not stand the child, never wanted to see him again, and

*Executive Director, National Committee for Prevention of Child Abuse, Suite 510, 111 E. Wacker, Chicago, Illinois 60601.

asked for an immediate placement for adoption. She was told that it would be impossible to relinquish her child so abruptly, that the child could not be placed that day, and that the parents would first need to become involved in relinquishment counseling. Two weeks later, David arrived at a hospital emergency room. He had been dead for at least 72 hours and had severe burns from the waist down.

CHILD ABUSE

Child abuse is not a recent phenomenon.[1] It was not until 1962, however, that child abuse was formally recognized as a widespread threat to the health and the lives of young children.[2] Originally termed "The Battered Child Syndrome," it was defined as a serious, nonaccidental *physical injury* to a child. On the basis of Kempe's work, it was estimated that there were 60,000 children battered each year. That proved to be a rather dramatic understatement.

During the last 15 years knowledge about child abuse has grown dramatically. As our knowledge has grown, the definition has grown accordingly. Child abuse today includes the elements of a nonaccidental physical injury, neglect, sexual molestation, and emotional abuse. Today, it is estimated that 665,000 to 1,675,000 children are physically abused, sexually molested, or seriously neglected each year.[3] At least 2,000 (and probably closer to 5,000) children die each year as a direct result of that abuse.[4] In most cases child abuse is not a single attack or a single act of deprivation. It is continual ongoing behavior. Its effects are cumulative. The longer the abusive behavior continues, the more severe are the injuries to a child.

FAMILY DYNAMICS IN CASES OF CHILD ABUSE

It is impossible to characterize abusing parents by the color of their skin, their ethnic heritage, their religious preference, or their wealth. The rather sad fact is that abusing parents come from all walks of life.

---

[1] See Radbill, 1969: The history of child abuse and infanticide. *In* C. H. Kempe and R. E. Helfer (eds.), The Battered Child. University of Chicago Press, Chicago.

[2] Kempe, H. 1962. The battered child syndrome. JAMA 181: 17.

[3] Light, R. 1973. Abused and neglected children in America: A study of alternative policies. Harvard Ed. Rev. 43: 66.

[4] Kempe, H. 1976. Predicting and preventing child abuse, establishing children's rights by issuing access to health care through the concept of a health visitor. Amer. J. Dis. Child.

There is no specific psychiatric diagnosis that encompasses all of the personality and behavioral patterns of parents who do abuse their children. There are, however, certain common patterns of child-parent relationships, or child-rearing practices that are indigenous to abuse.

> They (parents) share, however, a common pattern of parent-child relationships, or style of child-rearing characterized by a high demand for the child to perform so as to gratify the parents, and by the use of severe physical punishment to insure the child's proper behavior. Abusive parents also show an unusually high vulnerability to criticism, disinterest, or abandonment by the spouse or other important person, or to anything that lowers their already inadequate self-esteem. Such events create a crisis of unmet needs in the parent who then turns to the child with exaggerated demands for gratification. The child is often unable to meet such parental expectations and is punished excessively.
> Both this pattern of a demanding, aggressive behavior toward the child, and a crisis of emotional deprivation which triggers the pattern of abuse, stem directly from the parent's own childhood experience and learning. Abusive parents were raised in a similar system, i.e., or expected to perform well, to gratify parental needs very early in life, and then were criticized, punished, and often abused for failure to do so. They felt their own needs were neither met nor adequately considered; rather, they had to orient toward parental expectation and develop an almost intuitive understanding of what would satisfy the parents and prevent punishment. (It should be emphasized that while these factors are not abnormal or unusual in themselves, the degree to which they are expressed is distinctively excessive.)
> These childhood experiences are profound and provide lasting imprints which are revealed in the way adults feel about themselves and their children. Abusive parents have no basic, firm cushion of self esteem or awareness of being loved and valuable to carry them through periods of stress. Instead, they are in constant need of reassurance. They are inwardly shattered by anything that indicates poor performance resulting in disapproval from their spouse, relatives, employer, or any other person significant in their lives. In such a crisis of insecurity, they repeat what they learned in childhood about how parents behave and they turn to their own infant or child for the nurturing and reassurance they so sorely need to restore this sense of self esteem.[5]

Why child abuse takes place is a rather complex issue. It is likely to occur when four separate yet interrelated factors coalesce.[6]

---

[5] Steele, B. 1972. *In* C. H. Kempe and R. E. Helfer (eds.), Helping the Battered Child and His Family, p. 4. J. B. Lippincott, Philadelphia.

[6] For a more complete discussion of the diagnosis of child abuse, see: A Look at Child Abuse, The National Committee for Prevention of Child Abuse, Suite 510, 111 E. Wacker Drive, Chicago, Illinois 60601.

Adults have the potential to abuse. The potential may stem from their having been abused, neglected, or deprived as children, or when the parent has no friends, no neighbors, or relatives to turn to in times of crises. The parent frequently doesn't like himself, cannot meet his own emotional needs, and no one is present to provide emotional support. The parent with the potential to abuse almost always views the child with unrealistic expectations.

The parent views the child as special or different. The parent may "see" the child as being different or having special needs that sets the child apart from other children. What is important is not that the child is or is not different, but that the parent "sees" the child as being different or special. The child may be seen as too passive or too active. The parent may see in the child something the parent doesn't like about himself or herself. The child may be the result of an unwanted pregnancy. The child may have a birth defect.

There is a crisis or a series of crises. The crisis does not have to be major to precipitate abuse. An argument, a car that won't start, a crying baby, or an unwanted, unexpected visitor may be sufficient to exaggerate the loneliness and the frustration and trigger the abusive incident.

The parent is lonely and friendless. For all practical purposes the parent is isolated. He has no friends and no neighbors and no relatives to turn to in times of crises.

In any family, in any part of the country, given the right conditions child abuse can occur.

MANDATORY REPORTING

In the early 1960's a few states enacted into law mandatory reporting statutes. These early efforts required physicians to report suspected cases of child abuse in an attempt to identify the extent of the problem, the identity of the abusers, and the identity of the abused.

Today all 50 states, Puerto Rico, The Virgin Islands, and Washington, D.C. have adopted mandatory reporting statutes.[7] These mandatory reporting statutes are based upon the premises that: 1) Child abuse is a continuum. In the majority of cases child abuse is not a one-time occurrence. 2) The primary focus should be on the rather innocuous injuries, in an attempt to identify child abuse as quickly as possible. 3) In most cases

---

[7] Fraser, B. 1974. A pragmatic approach to child abuse. Amer. Crim. Law Rev. 12(1): 103.

the physician sees the child *after* serious injury has been inflicted and medical attention is necessary. As a result, most mandatory reporting statutes today not only require physicians to report, but they require all persons who come into contact with young children and who have an opportunity to identify injuries to report their suspicions. These statutes make a concerted effort to identify the child in peril as quickly as possible. The mandatory reporting statute delineates the responsibility of various individuals and organizations and creates a child abuse delivery system. In short, the mandatory reporting statute is the vehicle used to identify suspected cases of child abuse and provide entree into the health care and protective service system.

COLORADO'S MANDATORY STATUTE[8]

Unfortunately, every state has drafted and enacted into law its own mandatory reporting statute. This means that there are 50 different interpretations of abuse, 50 different interpretations of who must report, and 50 different interpretations of what must be done once a report of child abuse is made.[9] Although specifics do vary from state to state, there is a certain structural similarity between each state's mandatory reporting statute. For the purposes of this chapter, the author has chosen the Child Protection Act of Colorado. It has been chosen for three reasons: 1) it does have structural similarity to other states' mandatory reporting statutes and it will provide a focus for discussion; 2) it is probably the most innovative statute in existence today; and 3) it is a model which in all likelihood will be duplicated by other states. The purpose of the Child Protection Act is to identify the child in peril as quickly as possible, to provide protective services, and to try and keep the family unit intact, if possible.

Persons required to report suspected cases of child abuse in Colorado include: physician, child health associate, medical examiner or coroner, dentist, osteopath, optometrist, chiropractor, chiropodist or podiatrist, registered nurse or licensed practical nurse, hospital personnel engaged in the admission, care, or treatment of patients, Christian Science practitioner, school official or employee, social worker or worker in a family

---

[8] The Child Protection Act of 1976. Colorado Rev. Stat. Ann. § 19-10-101–19-10-118.

[9] See testimony, Brian G. Fraser before Select Committee on Education of the Committee on Education and Labor, House of Representatives, 93rd Congress, October 1, 1973.

care home or child care center, and mental health professional. Obviously, the public health nurse belongs to that larger, generic classification of nurses and is mandated by law, in Colorado, to report.

Colorado, like all other states, requires that cases of suspected child abuse (fiat accompli) be reported. Colorado, unlike most other states, also requires the reporting of conditions or circumstances that would reasonably result in abuse. It is important to know that what is required to be reported is a suspicion. It is not the responsibility of the reporter to definitively diagnose the suspected case. He or she is not required to investigate, and he or she is not required to develop the prognosis. There is no rule that definitively delineates *when* a report must be made. A common rule of thumb, however, is if there is a doubt, resolve that doubt in favor of the child and report.

Like most other states, Colorado requires that reports of suspected child abuse, or circumstances and conditions that would reasonably result in abuse, be made to the local Department of Social Services. Once a report of suspected child abuse has been received, it is the Department of Social Services' responsibility to investigate that report.

Colorado, like every other state, grants immunity from civil and criminal liability for persons reporting suspected cases of child abuse in good faith. To put it in slightly different terms, if someone who is mandated to report does report, in good faith, he or she cannot be held liable if that report eventually proves to be erroneous. Good faith means an honest belief.

Colorado, like 47 other states, has created a central registry[10] to house all reports of suspected child abuse. If the central registry is functioning properly, it can be used to help keep track of abusive parents who have a habit of doctor shopping and hospital shopping, for diagnostic purposes, for court purposes, and to evaluate the effectiveness of local Departments of Social Services.

Colorado, like some other states, allows physicians and hospitals to take color photographs and x-rays of trauma without parental permission, to assume temporary custody of the child if there is a reasonable cause to believe that the child has been abused and would be in danger if returned home, and provides the abused child with his own spokesman should the case proceed to court: the guardian ad litem.[11]

---

[10] For a more complete discussion of central registeries and how they may be utilized, see: Fraser, B. G. (1974). Toward a more practical central registry. Denver Law J. 51(4): 509.

[11] For a more complete discussion of the concept and how the guardian ad litem can be utilized by the public health nurse, see: Fraser, B. G. 1976. Independent representation for the abused and neglected child. Cal. West. Law Rev.

Colorado, unlike any other state, has mandated by law the creation of multi-disciplinary child protection teams to help provide a diagnosis, a prognosis, and coordinate treatment.[12] And finally, Colorado has recognized the need for treatment, not retribution, in cases of child abuse. It provides for the diversion of abusive parents out of the criminal court system into an acceptable treatment modality.

WHAT HAPPENS ONCE A REPORT OF SUSPECTED CHILD ABUSE IS MADE

There is in every state at least one agency that is mandated by law to investigate reports of suspected child abuse. That agency is usually the Department of Social Services, or its equivalent (Social and Rehabilitative Services, Children and Family Services, Protective Services, etc.). It is important to note that anyone can make a report of suspected child abuse. While it is true that certain individuals are mandated to report, that mandate does not preclude others from reporting voluntarily. Furthermore, the agency that is mandated to investigate reports of suspected child abuse cannot distinguish between reports made by those mandated to report and those who report on a voluntary basis. Nor can that agency differentiate between anonymous reports and reports in which the reporter identifies himself. The mandated agency must investigate every report of suspected child abuse.

Probably the easiest method to understand this rather complex process is to take a typical example and follow it through to adjudication. If a physician examines a child with numerous bruises and a fractured leg and if he believes that those injuries are nonaccidental in nature, he must, by law, report. In Colorado, the physician must report to the local Department of Social Services. In Colorado, the physician may assume temporary custody of the child, if he feels that the child has been abused and would be in danger if returned home.

Under Colorado law, the local Department of Social Services must make an immediate investigation. The purpose of that investigation is to determine whether or not the child has been abused and whether or not the child is *currently* in danger in his home environment. If, during the course of the investigation, the department feels that the child is in danger in his home environment, it may petition the court for temporary custody.

---

[12] For a complete discussion of how child protection teams function and how they have been integrated into the Colorado Statutes, see: Fraser, Colorado, Child Abuse and the Child Protection Act, The National Center, 1205 Oneida St., Denver, Colorado 80220.

At the completion of the investigation, the department must evaluate its data to determine if the child is currently in danger and if the child has been abused under state law. It is important to note that there may well be a difference between a danger to a child and what is considered child abuse under state law. In some states the definition of child abuse is drawn very narrowly. In those states the investigation may identify a child who is currently in danger, but whose injuries (or whose parents' behavior) could not be classified as child abuse under state law. In either case, intervention is necessary and imperative. If a child's injuries or the parents' behavior can be classified as child abuse under state law, it simply gives the mandated agency one other option for intervention and treatment—the Juvenile Court.

If the child's injuries or the parents' behavior can be classified as child abuse under state law, there may be a decision to file the case in the Juvenile Court. Juvenile Court proceedings are initiated with the filing of a *Petition.*[13] A petition is simply a piece of paper that alleges that the child has been abused and that the court does have jurisdiction to hear the case. The petitioner is the person, or agency, who files the petition. In most states it is the Department of Social Services that is the petitioner. The respondent is the person(s) who responds to the allegations made in the petition.

Juvenile Court proceedings may involve as many as four separate hearings. The first is the Advisement. At the Advisement hearing, the court formally indicates the allegations that have been made and notes the rights guaranteed to the respondents. The second is the Setting. At the Setting, a time and place is agreed upon by all parties to try the merits of the case. The third is the Adjudicatory Hearing. The purpose of the Adjudicatory Hearing is to determine whether or not the child's injuries or the parents' behavior can be classified as child abuse under state law. If the child's injuries or the parents' behavior cannot be classified as child abuse under state law, all legal proceedings cease. If the child's injuries or the parents' behavior is classified as child abuse under state law, the court will find the child neglected and will order a fourth, and final, hearing. The fourth hearing is called the Dispositional Hearing. At the Dispositional Hearing there is only one issue to resolve. That issue is who will be issued custody of the child. In Colorado (like most other states) the Juvenile Court has three options available to it. It may completely terminate the parent-child relationship, it may leave the child in his own home under court super-

---

[13] For a thorough discussion of how the juvenile court works, see: Besharov, Juvenile Justice Advocacy Practicing Law Institute, New York, 1974.

vision, or it may place the child in foster care. The last two options assume that there has been a favorable prognosis and require that another hearing be held within some fixed period of time. At that re-hearing, if treatment has been successful, the home environment will have stabilized and the court may formally withdraw.

ROLE OF THE PUBLIC HEALTH NURSE IN CASES OF CHILD ABUSE

In many cases, it is the public health nurse and not the physician or the social worker who first comes into contact with the potential child abuse case. In 35 states public health nurses are required by law to report cases of suspected child abuse. In *every* state the public health nurse has an ethical obligation to report suspected cases whether or not mandated by law. All public health nurses should have at least a working knowledge of child abuse, should know how child abuse is defined in that state, and should have a copy of that state's relevant statutes.

It is important to note, once again, that persons who are mandated to report are not mandated to make a complete investigation and to reach definitive diagnosis. The minimum responsibilities require that suspected cases of child abuse be reported. Unlike other potential reporters, however, the public health nurse has skills to make more than a cursory evaluation.

If there is an injury to a child which is suspicious, the public health nurse should be able to complete the following:

1. Carefully examine the injury and note it in the official record. Injuries should be noted and characterized according to their *type*, their *size* and *location*, their *severity*, and their *age*.
2. If a child is old enough to articulate for himself, he should be asked how the injury happened.
3. The parents should be asked in a friendly, nonthreatening manner for their explanation of the injuries. It is not advisable to cross-examine parents even if their explanation seems to be unreasonable.
4. It is advisable to inquire if the child has suffered other injuries during the past 12 to 24 months. It is a pattern of injuries over a period of time that is particularly indicative of child abuse.
5. It is prudent to try and determine if the parents are dealing with their children in a realistic manner.
6. It is prudent to try and determine if there has been some kind of crisis which might have precipitated the attack.
7. It is prudent to try and determine if the parents do have others whom they can turn to in times of crises.

Listed below are indications of particular concern when assessing the possibility of child abuse. If one or more of the following factors are present, it would be prudent to consider the possibility of inflicted trauma.

When the Parent[14]

1. Shows signs of loss of control, or fear of losing control.
2. Presents contradictory history concerning the nature of the injury.
3. Projects cause of injury onto a sibling or a third party.
4. Is unduly delayed in bringing the child in for care.
5. Shows detachment.
6. Reveals inappropriate awareness of the seriousness of the situation.
7. Continues to complain about irrelevant problems unrelated to the injury.
8. Personally is misusing drugs or alcohol.
9. Is disliked, for unknown reasons, by the physician or nurse.
10. Presents a history that cannot or does not explain the injury.
11. Gives specific "eyewitness" history of abuse.
12. Gives a history of repeated injury.
13. Has no one to "bail" him/her out when "uptight" with the child.
14. Is reluctant to give information.
15. Refuses to consent to further diagnostic studies.
16. Hospital "shops."
17. Cannot be located.
18. Is psychotic or psychopathic.
19. Has been reared in a "motherless" atmosphere.
20. Has unrealistic expectations of the child.

When the Child[14]

1. Has an unexplained injury.
2. Shows evidence of dehydration and/or malnutrition, without obvious cause.
3. Has been given inappropriate food, drink, and/or drugs.
4. Shows evidence of overall poor care.
5. Is unusually fearful.
6. Shows evidence of repeated injury.
7. "Takes over" and begins to care for parents' needs.

---

[14] Reprinted from: Helping the Battered Child and His Family, C. H. Kempe and R. E. Helfer (eds.), J. B. Lippincott, Philadelphia, p. 73.

8. Is seen as "different" or "bad" by the parents.
9. Is indeed different in physical or emotional makeup.
10. Is dressed inappropriately for the degree or type of weather.
11. Shows evidence of sexual abuse.
12. Shows evidence of repeated skin injuries.
13. Shows evidence of repeated fractures.
14. Shows evidence of "characteristic" x-ray changes to the long bones.
15. Has injuries that are not mentioned in the history.

If there is reasonable cause to believe that this might be child abuse, it must be reported to the appropriate agency immediately.

The public health nurse must be able to see child abuse as something more than the willful act of a cruel, depraved parent. She must understand that more is needed than a call for personal retribution. What is needed to correct the problem is not punishment, but treatment. Perhaps the greatest hurdle that she must clear in dealing with abusive parents and their children is the ability to hide her own emotions behind a cloak of objective and rational reasoning. The first reaction when confronted with child abuse may well be one of horror. The secondary reaction is often the feeling of a need for retribution. It should be noted, however, that this driving need for retribution is a need of the observer and not a need of the child. A prudent, reasonable approach to the problem of child abuse would seem to dictate the need for treatment.

In most cases the public health nurse is seen as a nonthreatening helpful individual. She has a natural entree into the home and can be instrumental in preventing child abuse through timely intervention. This natural entree is often possible when visiting the family for physical health reasons. Astute observations of the family dynamics are easily made, beginning with the first home visit, provided that the nurse is interested in family care and does not limit herself to specific health care procedures, i.e., throat cultures, temperature taking, etc. Taking the time to get a picture of family life style will yield positive results and conserve time and energy for all parties. Although it is true that large case loads are very often the greatest stumbling block in assessing a family's dynamics and needs, the nurse's expertise in assessment is many times all that is needed from her. Intervention may be as simple as knowing who or what in the community can assist this family with whatever stresses are indigenous to the individuals concerned. To do her job properly, the public health nurse must know what services and treatment are available within her community. If family needs are properly assessed it should be a relatively easy task to integrate the family needs into available services. Appropriate connections or outlets for a family in need may very well be the only preventive measure needed. It should be noted that appropriate outlets for the family needs are not always professional. In any event, persons or programs chosen to aid the family must be chosen carefully to avoid compounding, rather than helping, the problem.

Sometimes it is appropriate for the nurse to be involved on a telephone basis after the initial relationship has been established and a trusting situation exists. These therapeutic telephone contacts often resolve into a stage in which the patient only needs to know the nurse will be available when a crisis is again looming. The involvement may change again temporarily when a crisis is eminent and more direct contact is appropriate.

Besides the preventive role of public health nurses discussed in the above paragraphs, there is the helper role in a truly abusive family. The helper role may encompass a variety of assistances, depending upon a need. When a diagnosis of child abuse has been made, there is often an overwhelming feeling of shame and worthlessness felt by the parent. This feeling may be so stressful as to temporarily prevent adequate day-to-day function. Although therapy, either on a group or individual basis, may be necessary, it does not necessarily address itself to the myriad of other issues encountered during a day of living. A friend who is a willing listener, one who perhaps is available with a shoulder to cry on is, in many cases, a very real need for these parents.

Although it is true that the main issue in this chapter is child abuse, there are other related forms of this condition that may also result, in many instances, in developmental deviations to a greater or lesser degree. A nurse with a developmental orientation often has the opportunity to identify a problem more readily. Her concerns regarding a developmental problem, which may have been identified through the use of a screening tool, could very well lead to the recognition of a neglectful or depriving situation. The issues involved in these cases are identical with those of child abuse, but may differ in severity.

In summary, the commitment is truly long term and is variable with each family. Assessment and intervention must be an ongoing process for these families even when formal therapy has ceased.

WHERE TO TURN FOR HELP

In very few cases is the diagnosis of child abuse black or white. In the majority of cases the diagnosis of child abuse involves an inductive leap. The conclusion is based upon a physical examination of the child, an evaluation of the home environment, an evaluation of the parent-child relationship, and a careful examination of the parents' explanation for the injuries in terms of reasonableness. In many cases, additional information is invaluable in making a tentative diagnosis. In many cases it is wise to speak with a social worker who might have been previously involved with the family, a family physician, close relatives, or the next-door neighbor.

A large number of states have tacitly recognized the rather complex factors that must be assessed in evaluating a suspected case of child abuse. These states have created *multidisciplinary child protection teams* to aid in the diagnosis and prognosis and to provide a continuity of treatment. These multidisciplinary teams pool expertise in different fields. Weaknesses are minimized and the strengths are maximized. Colorado has become the first state to create these teams by statute, although virtually all states do have child protection teams. If there is a child protection team in the community, use it. It has dealt with the problem before and can provide expertise not readily available elsewhere. If a child protection team does not exist within your community, do not be hesitant to lean on other professionals who can lend their expertise to yours. Identify a physician, hospital personnel, a lawyer, a social worker, a police officer, or a mental health or public health facility that can be called in times of crises.

Copies of the state's mandatory reporting statute can be obtained from the local Department of Social Services, the local County Attorney's office, the local District Attorney's office, or a regional office of the Office of Child Development.

There are four national organizations that focus on particular aspects of child abuse. These organizations will, upon request, include you on their mailing lists. They have available publications which can increase your expertise.

The National Committee for Prevention of Child Abuse, Suite 510, 111 E. Wacker, Chicago, Illinois 60601.
  Primary focus: prevention, coordination, and use of volunteers.
The National Center for the Prevention and Treatment of Child Abuse and Neglect, 1205 Oneida Street, Denver, Colorado 80220.
  Primary focus: innovative treatment programs for the abused child and his family.
The American Humane Association, Children's Division, Post Office Box 1266, Denver, Colorado 80201.
  Primary focus: creating and approving protective services.
The National Center on Child Abuse and Neglect, Department of H.E.W. Post Office Box 182, Washington, D. C. 20013.

Primary focus: implementation of Public Law 93-247 to identify, treat, and prevent child abuse.

CONCLUSION

Child abuse hurts. Its most obvious victim is the child. It is, however, the whole community that suffers. Public health nurses have an ethical obligation to report all suspected cases of child abuse to the appropriate agency. In some states, public health nurses are mandated by law to report. It should always be kept in mind that the law requires reports of suspected child abuse. It does not require, nor does it encourage, that the reporter make his or her own investigation, develop his or her own diagnosis, or offer treatment. It is a deadly mistake to assume *personally* all of these responsibilities.

At the same time, it is noted that the public health nurse does have certain skills and expertise that sets her apart from other mandated reporters. These skills and that expertise can be utilized to aid the proper authorities in completing the investigation, reaching the proper diagnosis, developing the proper prognosis, and providing a certain continuity in treatment. The public health nurse is viewed as a caring, nonthreatening, supportive person. She is an ideal candidate to work effectively with potentially abusive and abusive parents. If she is properly trained, she can identify the needs of a family and she can identify the available resources within her community. Functioning properly, the public health nurse should be able to serve as a conduit into the health care delivery system, as well as serving in the capacity of a supportive therapeutic individual.

More importantly perhaps, the public health nurse can serve in a preventive role. If she is aware of the dynamics involved in the cases of child abuse and if she can properly assess the dynamics involved in a particular family, she should be able to mitigate against the injuries inflicted on a child. It is simply more prudent today to practice preventive medicine than it is to practice curative medicine. In a sophisticated, medically advanced community there is little value in utilizing an iron-lung when a Salk vaccine is available.

SUGGESTED READINGS: GENERAL

Kempe, H., and R. Helfer. 1972. Helping the Battered Child and His Family, J. B. Lippincott, Philadelphia.
Kempe, H., and R. Helfer. 1974. The Battered Child, Ed. 2. University of Chicago Press, Chicago.

Kempe, H., and R. Helfer. 1976. Child Abuse and Neglect: The Community and the Family. Ballinger, Cambridge, Mass.

Martin, H. 1976. Child Abuse: A Developmental Approach. Ballinger, Cambridge, Mass.

Schmitt, B. The Child Protection Team. Raven Press, New York.

Young. 1971. Wednesday's Children: Child Abuse and Neglect in New York. McGraw-Hill Book Co., New York.

Helfer, R., B. Caulfield, and T. Hanrahan. A Look at Child Abuse, The Naional Committee for Prevention of Child Abuse, Suite 510, 111 E. Wacker Drive, Chicago, Illinois 60601.

SPECIALIZED READINGS

Child Abuse Legislation

Fraser, B. 1974. A pragmatic approach to child abuse. Amer. Crim. Law Rev. 12(1): 103.

Sussman and Cohen. 1975. Reporting Child Abuse and Neglect. Ballinger, Cambridge, Mass.

Nonaccidental Physical Injury

Schmitt, B., and H. Kempe. 1975. The pediatrician role in child abuse and neglect. Curr. Probl. Pediatr. Vol. 5.

Neglect

Wald, M. 1975. State intervention on behalf of neglected children. Stan. Law Rev. 27(4): 985.

XIII ON BECOMING A HELPER

Jane E. Chapman, R.N., Ph.D*

All of the material within the previous chapters has been presented to assist health care workers to be more effective helpers. Yet we all know that in spite of our well intentioned efforts to learn more facts and to apply our new-found knowledge, something often goes askew in our helping relationships with patients and their families. In our growth and development as professionals, we have all experienced patients who "do not act the way they should," or those who do not perceive themselves to have been helped at all. At other times, one finds that certain patients indeed perceive a situation to be helpful, but upon follow-up the critical "help" which the patient perceived is quite different from that which one believed was being provided.

To gain a clear perspective as to what happens, or fails to happen, when patients and health care workers come together, let us explore some observations about "helping." First, most professional curricula for health care workers do not teach "how to help" as a generalizable process which applies across all professional disciplines and various health care settings, irrespective of the problems of the patient. To the chagrin of health care students and new professionals, they often find themselves loaded with the products of scientific knowledge in the form of facts, tests, and treatment recommendations, but meagerly prepared to set the occasion with patients for a helping process to occur. As well, it is observed that many health care workers are more preoccupied with disciplinary differences and specialty offerings than with a fuller understanding of their interdisciplinary responsibility: to help those who seek health care in the most meaningful way possible.

Individuals and families, on the other hand, expect that the professionals whom they encounter will know how to help them. From all walks

*Assistant Clinical Professor of Clinical Psychology, University of Colorado Medical Center, Denver, Colorado; Private Practice, Clinical and Consulting Psychology, Denver, Colorado.

of life, and of varying chronological age, each person who seeks professional help has general notions of what to expect from our health care system. In addition, within each individual's frame of reference about self and relationships with the world, unique notions exist about what one wants help to be and when one's particular life space once again "feels right." Without some way for health care workers and patients to maximize the possibility for getting on the same wavelength when they interact, it is little wonder that helping is often perceived by both parties as an ill-defined, hit or miss affair.

THE HELPER AS AN EVALUATOR

An effective helping process in any health care setting involves the bringing together of the assets of the health care system, the individual health care worker, and the individual patient or family. Overall, if helping is to be a safe, humanistic process—respectful of what patients want for themselves—it is critical that helpers be accurate evaluators.

To be an accurate evaluator, one needs considerable knowledge in detecting evidence of deviations from physical and emotional health. This implies that one needs to have considerable diagnostic know-how. However, being a good diagnostician is not synonymous with being a good evaluator. Evaluation is a more holistic concept, the process of which necessitates a total person view of another. Such a total person view includes appraisal of a patient's goals, aspirations, and assets *as well as* temporary or permanent physical, emotional, or social liabilities. This difference between "evaluating" and "diagnosing" is critical to understand as it is within a broader, often subjectively laced knowledge about patients and their families that one finds the key to a patient's motivation to seek health and live productively. It is also from this broader knowledge that one begins to understand what influences a patient's resistance to healthful ways or "giving up" processes which often lead to a patient's physical or emotional death. An accurate diagnosis is always crucial, but it has no meaning in terms of ultimate help to a patient unless there is a full understanding of what the patient can or wants to do about it.

Being a good evaluator requires that health care workers become *interpersonally effective* in "getting where patients are at." One does not do this by simply running a patient through screening devices or technological tests of physical function, even though such procedures may be absolutely critical to the helping situation. To fully evaluate and to obtain the rich data that the patient's subjective self can and must provide if help is to be safe and meaningful, patients (or their representatives) must be allowed to "tell it how it is." This is not the easiest task in the world in some situations even for the behavioral "expert," but neither is it as hard as it might seem. Let us first explore some of the factors which often get in the way of getting to know patients.

ROADBLOCKS TO KNOWING PATIENTS

Roadblocks to getting "where patients are at" tend to fall within three categories: those variables which are to be found within the health care system, those which are found within the person of the health care worker, and those which are found within the person of the patient.

System variables which deter a meaningful evaluation of those who seek us out are well known. In some health care settings the environment is so chaotic and unresponsive to humane considerations of either patients or staff that it is literally impossible for two people to relate effectively and learn about each other. Often the press to "get them in and get them out" is so great that concern for whether or not helping has occurred is not a relevant issue. In less chaotic, more organized settings, well meaning but poorly focused health care workers may convey an attitude of "we know best" and, in spite of the time spent with patients and families, the system atmosphere does not begin with "where the help-seeker is at," nor does it ever allow that point to be reached.

Closer observation of the "we know best" atmosphere generally finds that within the nature of the health care workers in such settings is a poorly integrated model of interpersonal skill and high reliance upon policy; i.e., because so many health care workers have not been taught to explore with patients beyond traditional diagnostic issues, it is more comfortable to rely on mechanistic procedures. This kind of defensive posture, as reflected in health care practice, leads to shutting out patients' personal input, to patient perceptions that no one is listening, and to stereotypic procedures within which everyone is treated the same.

From the understanding of people in general, one can also appreciate the roadblocks which exist within patients when they seek us out. For example, few people, irrespective of age or the social setting in which they are encountered, will tell "just anybody" everything upon first encounter. All of us humans must come to trust another and be convinced that the other person will do right by us before we make visible "who we are." In professional helping, development of trust with patients or their families will not come about simply because one holds a title or wears a uniform. This is particularly so in the past few years when the general public is more, rather than less, wary of the health care made available to them.

In addition to the generalized "stranger anxiety" which most humans experience in new encounters, most of our patients seek us out during the circumstances of heightened physical and emotional stress. Nondefensive verbal behaviors which might characterize a patient or family in a state of health may become obliterated as the effects of their illness or emotional turmoil take their toll. Some patients may never have been known to be forthright and verbal in expressing hopes, fears, or goals which give immediately visible clues as to what they think and feel. At other times, people who were once perceived to be cooperative and "easy to get along with" in everyday life suddenly become irritable and "difficult patients" to satisfy.

For most people who become patients when they step inside a health care setting, anxiety is reduced and the potential for knowing them is heightened when: 1) ambiguity about the setting is quickly dispelled, 2) expectations they hold are clarified early, 3) mutual goals between helper and patient (or their representatives) are set with the open understanding of the opportunity for on-going renegotiation, and 4) follow-up is assured. A useful helping model within which these four steps have a high degree of being accomplished is that of *advocacy*.

THE HELPER AS AN ADVOCATE

Advocacy is a concept which has been around for a long time in a variety of helping disciplines. It expresses that *one acts in behalf of another to the extent that the other person does not have the resources to act on one's own.* As adapted to the health care field, this position requires that the helper be a good listener as to what patients express, and one *early* evaluates: 1) whether the patients are in the most appropriate setting for the care they seek, 2) whether patients are utilizing the best resource (health care worker) within that setting, 3) what the helper-seekers' strengths might be in resolving their own problems, and 4) what is getting in the way of patients utilizing their own resources, i.e., those factors which lie within the patient, within the helper, or within the total system in which both patients and helpers find themselves.

The evaluative posture which is integrated within an advocacy model requires open communication with patients. For example, a health care advocate very early communicates with patients about what can or cannot be expected realistically from the relationship and the setting. This approach has several payoffs. From research we learn that when one person in a dyad discloses more about himself, the other party is more likely to trust than distrust and subsequently lets the other know more about who they are. Therefore, health care advocates who begin with a realistic, informative relationship with patients—neither overpromising or under-valuing what they have to offer—find that patients tend to be more disclosing of themselves. Because an advocate is realistic concerning initial and on-going expectations, one also finds that patient dependency upon others to "do it all" is reduced, as well as finding that there is less angry insistence that the helper is an all-fulfilling god.

Goal setting in an advocacy relationship is an open, negotiated process with patients or their representatives. It is characterized by mutuality, respect, and flexibility. The helper maturely understands that there are many factors which may be getting in the way of a patient's or family's expressions of their problems, fears, goals and what they think needs to be done about the dilemma. Advocates struggle *with* their patients to arrive at beginning and on-going goals. They consistently listen to the feedback of patients as to how things are going, and they are sensitive to when this feedback signals the necessity of negotiating new goals. Obviously, the advocacy attitude of helping does not allow the helper to "take over." Just as the advocate does not "put down" the input from patients or their representatives, the advocate does not go beyond that which help seekers want or can do for themselves.

Because the advocacy attitude stresses "in behalf of" behaviors, health care advocates are sensitive to continuity of care issues. For example, if a specific helper or agency is determined as not the most appropriate to a patient's or family's needs, the advocate does not abandon them. The helper continues to act in the patient's behalf in seeing that more appropri-ate resources are found. The effective health care advocate therefore must be knowledgeable of the local and regional resources, and acts as a coordinative broker in seeing that patients get to the right place with minimum chaos and maximum orientation as to what to expect.

Finally, advocacy as a helping model also stimulates an undying curiosity as to how patients have progressed when it has been mutually determined that they can "go it on their own." This curiosity is more than a concern for any one patient's welfare; it also acknowledges that evaluation of the outcome of one's own helping behavior is of equal importance. Only if we have the courage and professional integrity to find out how our patients have perceived their experience with us can we determine whether or not we are effective helpers and what are our needs for continuing education.

SUGGESTED READINGS

Carkuff, R. 1969. Helping and Human Relations. Holt, Rinehart, and Winston, New York.

Chapman, J. E., and H. H. Chapman. 1975. Behavior and Health Care: A Humanistic Helping Process. The C. V. Mosby Company, St. Louis.

Kahn, A. J., S. B. Kamerman, and B. G. McGowan. 1972. Child Advocacy Report on a National Baseline Study. Columbia University School of Social Work, New York.

Jourard, S. M., and P. E. Jaffe. 1970. Influence of an interviewer's disclosure on the self-disclosing behavior of interviewees. J. Counsel. Psychol. 17(3): 252–257.

Rubin, Z. 1974. Lovers and other strangers: The development of intimacy in encounters and relationships. Amer. Sci. 62: 182–189.

INDEX

Abdomen in physical examination, 24
Abortions, spontaneous, 54
Achondroplasia, 66
Alleles, 65
Amniocentesis, 61, 64
Anencephalic children, 49
Anencephaly, 80, 82
Anomaly, congenital, 82
Anoxia, 81
Anus in physical examination, 25
Appearance, general, in screening for developmental problems, 19
Articulation and sucking, 132–133
Artificial insemination, 67
Asphyxia, 81
Audiogram, 86
  threshold, 126
Audiometry, pure tone screening, 125
Auditory behavior, maturation of, 122
Auditory defects, high risk register, 87
Autosomes, 57
  chromosome abnormalities involving, 63

Babbling, 135
Babinski reflex, 27
Back in physical examination, 26
Background information in screening for developmental problems, 7–13
Baseline, definition, 163
Bayley Scales, 118
Behavior modification
  fading out the manipulation, 170
  use with children, 161–175

Bilirubin, serum, 82
Birth
  abnormal presentation, 83
  forceps deliveries, 83
  postmature, 83
Birth history in screening for developmental problems, 9–10
Birth weight, low, 80
Breathing
  as autonomic neuromuscular activity, 133–134
  patterns, 133
Bronchopulmonary dysplasia, 81

Central nervous system, development of basic components of, 49
Cephalocaudal progression, 89
Cerebral palsy, high risk register, 87
Cesarean section, 83
Chest in physical examination, 23–24
Child abuse
  Colorado's mandatory statute, 181–183
  family dynamics in cases of, 178–180
  family history of, 85
  mandatory reporting, 180–181
  role of public health nurse in cases of, 177–191
  where to turn for help, 188–190
Chromosomes, 55–64
  disorders of, 59–64
  prevention of, 64
  X or Y, 63
Cleft lip and palate, 76
Clinic, high risk infant, 86

Color blindness, criteria for referral
for, 106
Color deficiencies, procedures for
testing for, 106
Communication, growth of, 131
Conception, timing of, 54
Convulsions, 84
Counseling
preconceptual, 54
reassurance, 54
Cyanosis, 84
Cystic fibrosis, 68

Deafness
congenital, 112
family history of, 86
Death, perinatal, 81
Denver Articulation Screening
Exam, 42
Denver Audiometric Screening
Test, 42
Denver Developmental Screening
Test, 4, 27, 32, 33–42, 85,
118
scoring of, 37
Denver Eye Screening Test, 42
Deoxyribonucleic acid, 55
Development
feeding, 144–145
normal and abnormal, 90
normal motor, in infant, 89–99
physical and genetic factors in
delayed, 151
prevention of problems in, 47–54
screening for problems in, 1–5,
7–13, 15–29, 31–45
Developmental Screening
Inventory, 85
Diabetes, maternal, 83
Diagnosis, prenatal, 71
Diet
of infant, 142–145
of preschool child, 146–147
Disorders
determined by a single defective
gene, 64–75

dominantly inherited, 65–68
methods of prevention of,
67–68
polygenic, 75
recessively inherited, 68–75
prevention of, 71
X-linked, 71–75
Down's syndrome, 59
Drug exposure of prospective
parents, 53
Duchenne muscular dystrophy, 71

Ears in physical examination, 21–22
Eclampsia, 83
Embryo
development of, 47, 48–50
critical stages, 50
prevention of developmental
problems, 47–54
Embryology
development chart, vi
relevance to child health, 47
Encephalitis, 84
Environment of prospective
parents, 52–54
Extensor tone in infant, 89
Extinction, definition of, 162
Extremities in physical examination, 25–26
Eyes in physical examination,
20–21

Face in physical examination,
20–22
Failure to thrive, 83
Family dynamics in child abuse
cases, 178–180
Far-sightedness, procedures for
testing, 105
Fetal development chart, viii
Fetus, evidence of distress of, 82
Fine motor-adaptive skills in DDST,
35, 36–37
Fisting, 98
excessive, 98

Flexor tone in infant, 89
Food habits
    of preschool child, 147–148
    of school-age child, 148
Food intake, child's, factors
        affecting, 149
Funny looking kid, 84

Gene
    dominant, 65
    recessive, 65
Gene locus, 67
Genetic disorders, 55–77
    family history, 9
Genetics of some common
        congenital malformations,
        75–76
Genitalia in physical examination,
        24–25
Gesell Infant Scales, 85
Gonadotropin, human chorionic,
        49

Handicap, preceding high risk
        factors, 79
Head in physical examination, 20
Hearing, importance of, to
        language, 132
Hearing loss
    early detection of, 111
    profound, early, 115
    sensorineural, 125
Hearing screening
    guidelines for, in infant,
        preschool, and school-age
        child, 111–130
    in infants, methods of, 114–124
    pure tone, of young child,
        125–128
    reasons for conducting programs
        for young children, 124–129
    reasons for instituting programs
        for infants, 112–113
Heart in physical examination,
        23–24

Heart disease, congenital, 76
Helper
    as an advocate, 196–197
    on becoming, 193–198
    as an evaluator, 194–195
Hemophilia A, 71
Hemorrhage, antepartum, 80
High risk infant: see Infant, high
        risk
High risk registry, 86
    and hearing screening of
        newborn, 114–116
History, family, of high risk infants,
        79–80
Home assessment, 152–155
Home Start, 156
Home visit vs. diagnostic clinic
        evaluation of developmental
        problems, 1–5
Homologues, 64
Hunter's syndrome, 74
Huntington's chorea, 65
Hydrocephaly, 79
Hyperopia, procedures for testing,
        105
Hyperthyroidism, maternal, 59
Hypoglycemia in pregnant woman,
        53–54
Hypotonicity, infant, 133
Hypoxia, 81

Identification, early
    of abnormal movement patterns,
        90
    of high risk infants, 79
Infant
    guidelines for hearing screening
        of, 111–130
    high risk, 79–87
        environmental factors, 84–85
        follow-up of, 85–87
        neonatal factors, 82
        postnatal factors, 84
        prenatal factors, 80
    neurological aspects of physical
        examination, 26–27

Infant—*continued*
  normal motor development in,
    89–99
  reasons for hearing screening
    programs for, 112–113
Intervention
  early, with high risk infants, 79
  preconceptual
    opportunities for, 51–54
    rationale for, 47–48

Jitteriness, 98

Kernicterus, 82

Landau reaction, 91–98
Language
  expressive, 135–138
  milestones, 136–138
  receptive, 134–135
Language ability of deaf children,
    111
Language development, 131–139
  critical periods for, 112
  delayed, 86
Language function, receptive and
    expressive, 132
Language skills in DDST, 35, 37
Language training, auditory, oral,
    or manual, 111
Linkage groups, 67
Localization, 119
Lungs in physical examination, 23
Lymph nodes in physical
    examination, 19–20

Malformations
  of central nervous system, 80
  common congenital, genetic
    aspects, 75–76
  congenital, family history of
    previous, 80
Manipulation, definition of, 163

Manipulative behavior, 135
Maternal-child interaction with high
    risk infants, 86
Meconium staining, 82
Meningitis, 84
Meningomylocele, 49
Mental retardation
  high risk register, 87
  incidence of, 63
Metabolic disease, family history
    of, 80
Microcephaly, 84
Milestones, developmental, 10
Milk, facts about, 145
Monosomies, partial, 63
Moro reflex, 91
Mother-Child Home Program, 157
Mother-child interaction, poor, 85
Motor development, normal, in
    infant, 89–99
Motor patterns, oral, 134
Motor skills, gross, in DDST, 35, 37
Mouth in physical examination, 22
Muscle imbalance, procedures for
    testing, 106–108
Muscular dystrophy, Duchenne's,
    family history of previous, 80
Mutation, 74

Neck in physical examination,
    22–23
Neural tube, closure of, 49
Neurofibromatosis, 65
Neurological aspects in physical
    examination, 26–28
Neurological examination of high
    risk infant, 85
Newborn, hearing screening,
    114–117
Nondisjunction, 58, 59
Nose in physical examination, 22
Nurse
  public health, role in child abuse
    cases, 177–191
  screening for developmental
    problems, 1–5, 7–13, 15–29,
    31–45

Nursing assessments, screening for
    developmental problems, 1–5,
    7–13, 15–29, 31–45
Nutrition
  and the child, 141–150
  during child's first year, 141
  counseling of prospective mother,
    53
  status and habits of prospective
    parents, 53

Oral-pharyngeal movements, 134
Orientation response, 118
Otitis media, 116
  as cause of hearing loss in
    school-age children, 124
  serous, 128
Otosclerosis, 116
Otoscopy, pneumatic, 125,
    128–129

Paramedical personnel, role in
    genetics, 76–77
Parents, prospective
  appraisal of environmental status
    of, 52–54
  appraisal of medical status of,
    51–52
  endocrine status, 52
  genital *Mycoplasmic* infection, 52
  infectious disease, 52
Perinatal complications, 151
Personal-social skills, DDST, 35–36
Phenotype, 65
Phenylketonuria, 70, 84
Physical examination
  approaches and suggested
    sequences, 17–18
  outline, 19–29
  in screening for developmental
    problems, 15–29
  techniques of, 16
  tools of, 16
  use of outline, 16–17
Polydactyly, 65
Polyhydramnios, 82

Preconceptual period, 48
Pregnancy
  health of mother during, 48
  history of, in screening for
    developmental problems, 7–9
Prematurity, 80
Prenatal care, 48
Ptosis, 65
Punishment, definition of, 161

Radiation, maternal exposure to,
    59
Reflexes
  early, 89
  in infant
    asymmetrical tonic neck reflex,
      90
    body righting on body reaction,
      91
    crossed extension, 90–91
    downward legs, 98
    foot grasp, 90
    hand grasp, 90
    head righting reaction, 91
    Landau reaction, 91–98
    major, 92–95
    midbrain righting reactions,
      91–98
    Moro, 91
    parachute, 98
    placing reaction, 91
    positive supporting reaction, 91
    primary, 89
    primitive, 90
    protective extension, 98
    protective reactions, 98
    "red flags," as concerns for
      later development, 98
    rooting, 90
    stepping, 91
    sucking, 90
    symmetrical tonic neck reflex,
      91
    tonic labyrinthine, 91
Reinforcement, definition of, 161
Retrolental fibroplasia, 81
Rubella, maternal, 80

School problems, families with
    children at risk for, 151–159
Scissoring, 98
Screening
    for developmental problems, 1–5,
        7–13, 15–29, 31–45
    for familial disorders, 51
    hearing
        guidelines for infant,
            preschool, and school-age
            child, 111–130
        for older infant in office and
            well-baby clinic, 117–124
    mass, 32
    multiphasic, 32
    multiple, 32
    preconceptual, rationale for,
        47–48
    selection, 33
    selective, 32
    single unit, 101
    vision, 101–109
        multiphasic, 101
Secondary sex characteristics, 64
Secretor, 67
Shaping, definition of, 162
Sickle cell anemia, 68
Skin in physical examination, 19
Speech
    critical periods for developing
        motor aspects of, 135
    milestones, 136–138
Speech development, 131–139
Spermiogenesis, 52
Spina bifida, 82
Stillbirths, 80
Stimulation, educational, 152
Submucous cleft, 116
Sucking and articulation, 132–133
Support system for family vs.
    isolation, 4–5
Sweep-check test, 127

Tay-Sachs disease, 68
    family history of previous, 80
Thalidomide, 53
Throat in physical examination, 22
Tools, screening, 31–45
Toxemia of pregnancy, 83
Toxoplasmosis, 80
Toy Demonstrator, 157
Translocation, 60
Translocation carrier, 63, 64
Trisomies, partial, 63
Trisomy 21, 59
Trophoblast cells, 49

Vision, peripheral, 118
Vision screening, 101–109
    room set-up, 102
Visual acuity, central, procedures
    for testing, 102–105
Visual defects, high risk register, 87
Vitamins, supplemental, 145
Vocalizations, 124
    as prespeech patterns, 134
    verbal responses from parents,
        131
Von Willebrand's disease, 65

Well-baby clinic, screening for older
    infant in, 117–124

X-rays of prospective mother, 53

Zinc, nutrition of prospective
    parents, 53
Zygote, 57